During my 30-plus years of pastoral ministry, I have had the privilege of answering many Bible-related questions. Without a doubt, the most common questions relate to heaven and eternity. It is with much joy that I now have a trusted source to recommend—Agnes Lawless's *Heaven, Our Glorious Home.* Agnes is a gifted storyteller and a true student of the Scriptures. Her book has the depth that anyone in academia would respect, and it contains the warmth and engagement that the layperson will appreciate. Do not miss this precious book!

Rev. Fred Williams

Lead Pastor, Snohomish Community Church, Snohomish, WA

Agnes Lawless writes from a rare perspective, drawing upon her experience in global missions with her feet fixed on the foundation of God's Word. She describes the reality of heaven, our eternal home, in a way that satisfies our understanding and the yearnings of our hearts. While reading *Heaven, Our Glorious Home,* you'll be thankful that Agnes chose this topic as the most recent subject of her research and creativity.

Rev. Fred Zoeller

Pastor, Westminster Presbyterian Church (PCA), Everett, WA

Could you use a little taste of heaven? Then treat yourself to a copy of *Heaven, Our Glorious Home* by Agnes Lawless and be transported to realms of glory! Through careful gleaning of Scripture, Agnes lays out a surprising number of detailed answers to our most pressing questions, including what heaven is like, if we will recognize one another, and what we will be doing there. One thing's certain, she will whet your appetite to see it for yourself!

Clint Kelly

Best-selling author of *The Landing Place* and *Escape Underground*

Many common notions about heaven—such as St. Peter guarding the Pearly Gates and humans becoming winged angels who play harps on Cloud 9—are found nowhere in Scripture. But now, in *Heaven, Our Glorious Home,* Agnes Lawless provides a clear, organized, exhilarating review of what the Bible actually says about our ultimate destination. This key resource belongs on every pastor's bookshelf.

Diana Savage
Author of *52 Heart Lifters for Difficult Times*

Heaven, Our Glorious Home tells us what the Bible has to say about the eternal joys awaiting those who love God. The truth is more fantastic than any of the fictions we humans construct for ourselves.

Joan Rawlins Biggar
Author of *Logger's Daughter: Growing Up in Washington's Woods*

Wonder filled my heart as I read *Heaven, Our Glorious Home.* I learned more about the beauties of heaven and the joys we'll experience in God's presence. I now have a better understanding of what heaven will be like, a greater longing for heaven, and a deeper yearning to live there for eternity with my Lord and Savior.

Sylvia Stewart
Missionary to Africa for thirty-two years and author of *Seattle Rayne* and *Kondi's Quest*

Heaven
Our Glorious Home
Amazing Answers to Our Questions

Agnes C. Lawless

Ferncliff Press

ISBN 978-1-7325671-0-8

Published by Ferncliff Press. Contact agneslaw@comcast.net

Book and cover design by Stewart Design, https://StewartDesign.studio

In memory of
my beloved father, Allan Cunningham Sr.,
and to
my loving second mother, Elizabeth Norton

OTHER BOOKS BY
AGNES C. LAWLESS

Aglow in the Kitchen, with Ann Thomas

Captivated by God, with Eadie Goodboy

The Drift into Deception

Keys to God's Heart, with Harriet Salathe

A Place for God to Live

Then and Now, with Richard Elkins

Under His Wings

The Word, with Eadie Goodboy

Table of Contents

FOREWORD

By Fred Zoeller

My friend Tom was an active person who enjoyed mountain climbing, skiing, hunting, fishing, and other sports. "Why would I want to go to heaven?" he asked me. "I'm not interested in sitting on a cloud with angels and plucking harp strings. Walking streets of gold doesn't interest me, either."

Perhaps Christians have unintentionally contributed to Tom's misunderstanding. We portray heaven's citizens as singing praises to God forever. We seem to think the only way to glorify God in heaven would be through spiritual activities.

Rarely do we describe eternity as an adventure God planned for us to enjoy. Would Tom be interested if he realized that in heaven he could travel through space and time, observing all creation? What if Tom could watch God form mountains or could see climbers ascend Mount Everest?

Here on earth we can glorify God in everything we do. For instance, in a biology lab at the Georgia Institute of Technology, when I gazed through a binocular microscope to identify the internal organs of a simple earthworm, a three-dimensional world opened up that I had never seen before. I located the worm's stomach, digestive track, brain, and five beating hearts. Before that moment, I wouldn't have shed a tear if a robin had jerked that earthworm out of the ground and gobbled it up. But now I saw the order, function, and beauty on display within the tiny creature itself. Awed by the Creator's handiwork, I praised God.

Watching an Olympic athlete perform or seeing a panoramic view unfold from the crest of a mountain range gives us glimpses of the expanded horizons of an eternal heaven. Eternity will vastly increase the ways we can glorify God.

God, the Creator, is unlimited by space and time.

God not only created the stars and planets, but he also created the energy that drives their activities. He manipulates space, appearing in our world or disappearing whenever he chooses. He showed himself to Adam and Eve, Moses, Abraham, Jacob, Daniel, Paul, and other biblical characters.

On two different occasions after his resurrection, Jesus walked through the walls of a locked room to spend time with his disciples. When he sat at a table with two believers in Emmaus, "their eyes were opened and they recognized him, and he disappeared from their sight" (Luke 24:31). Then as he ascended from earth, he vanished into the clouds.

The changeless God is also eternal. Since he is outside of time, time does not limit or affect him.

Physicists use physical laws and mathematical equations to describe the characteristics of our universe and how they relate to each other. Physicists don't include God in their laws and equations because they can't observe a spirit being. But they can closely observe space, time, matter, and energy. These elements, all connected, affect each other and fit into physicists' calculations.

Albert Einstein's theory of relativity describing how space, time, matter, and energy relate to each other was so accurate that it served as the basis for our development of atomic energy. The destruction of a tiny amount of matter releases such an immense amount of energy that it can power a city or produce a nuclear explosion.

If God is not limited by what he created, does this mean that he controls his creation? Of course, he does. The sovereign Creator manipulates space, time, matter, and energy any way he chooses.

Our resurrected bodies will be similar to Christ's.

After Jesus rose from the dead, he had a new physical body. He breathed, ate bread and fish, and drank just as before. His disciples personally witnessed that fact. But how could Jesus suddenly appear through walls and disappear again at will?

Every atom consists of subatomic particles separated by space—more space than actual matter. With only a slight change in the laws of atomic physics, atoms could take advantage of all that room and pass through each other. Who knows what changes God will make as he gives us spiritual bodies with the same capabilities as the resurrected body of Jesus Christ? Defying the law of gravity, Christ ascended into heaven. The Bible specifically says that we will receive bodies like Christ's. Perhaps our bodies will defy gravity too.

The apostle Paul said, "But our citizenship is in heaven. And we eagerly await a Savior from there, the Lord Jesus Christ, who, by the power that enables him to bring everything under his control, will transform our lowly bodies so that they will be like his glorious body" (Philippians 3:20–21). In 1 Corinthians 15, Paul describes resurrected bodies as spiritual. So our bodies, like Christ's, will be physical and spiritual at the same time.

Eternity includes a new heaven and earth.

The Bible says that God will renew and redeem all of creation. The Old and New Testaments both speak of a new heaven and earth. Isaiah 66:22 says, " 'As the new heavens and the new earth that I make will endure before me,' declares the LORD, 'so will your name and descendants endure.'" When Adam sinned, he brought about the fall of all creation. But redeemed humankind will enjoy a renewed creation and give glory to the Creator as originally intended.

In what ways will we enjoy that new heaven and earth? We have not only imagined deep-space travel, but we have also taken the first steps. People have already walked on the moon and sent spacecraft through the solar system. We have built an international space station and are planning travel to other planets and stars. In fact, our rover named Curiosity landed on Mars on August 5, 2012, to study the Red Planet.

Won't it be fun if our new capabilities will allow us to visit the entire universe? We could closely observe and understand every detail of God's renewed creation, from the stars to black holes, and give glory and honor to the Creator.

It is possible that these capabilities will allow Tom and the rest of us to observe every work of God from the foundation of this world, from the biblical to the scientific. We will fall on our knees and worship God in the way he intended when he first created the heavens and the earth.

I trust that this book will help you to better prepare for an eternity in heaven. May the quality of your life and service here have a real bearing on your happiness and reward over there.

Westminster Presbyterian Church (PCA)
Everett, Washington

ACKNOWLEDGEMENTS

Many thanks go to the members of my group of professional writers who critiqued the chapters carefully, asking questions, adding suggestions, and giving encouragement—Diana Savage, Joan Husby, Sylvia Stewart, Ginger Kauffman, and Dr. Marjorie Stewart, former English professor at Northwest University. Special thanks go to Diana for her fine editorial skills.

I also am grateful for the godly and gifted husbands God has given me, all of whom I first knew when I was with Wycliffe Bible Translators.

My first, John W. Lawless, spent four years in the US Navy and attended Bowdoin College, the University of North Dakota, and graduated from Moody Bible Institute. In the Philippines, he was the shortwave radio specialist, who kept contact with translators. He later graduated from the University of Washington and was a beloved teacher for many years. Our experience in a church was the background for my book, *The Drift into Deception.*

When John passed away from cancer, I later married our friend, Dick Elkins, whom we knew in the Philippines. Dick had graduated from Westmont College and received his PhD in linguistics from the University of Hawaii. Since he had translated the New Testament into Western Bukidnon Manobo, he checked a translation of the Old Testament into that language. While he worked, I edited and coauthored his book, *Then and Now: God's Sovereignty in the Lives of Two Bible Translators in the Philippines.* Then he said,

"I've accomplished two goals—checking the Old Testament and getting our book published. I wonder what God has for me now?" Three months later, after only two years of our marriage, he passed away from multiple melanoma.

Having outliving two husbands, I expected to be a widow the rest of my days. But God apparently had other ideas. Another friend from our years in the Philippines, Daniel Weaver, lost his wife, Marilou, after a long illness. Our mutual friend, Jo Shetler (author of *And the Word Came with Power*), told me of his loss. So I wrote him a note of sympathy, which eventually led to our marriage. He has edited and made valuable suggestions for this book, and we also have been working together on his devotional manuscript.

Dan is well qualified for our writing ministry. He not only graduated from Philadelphia College of Bible (now Cairn University) and Wheaton College, but he also did graduate work at Dallas Theological Seminary and the University of North Dakota and received his MEd at the University of Pittsburgh. He spent many years as Wycliffe's director in the Philippines and Asia, then of the Summer Institute of Linguistics' center in Dallas, as well as being international chaplain. He finally served as an interim pastor for several years.

I am also grateful for the ministry of the Reverend Fred Zoeller of Westminster Presbyterian Church (PCA), when my husband, John, was ill. He conducted a memorable memorial service, complete with a bagpiper playing, "Amazing Grace." I also appreciate the excellent foreword he wrote for this book.

Finally, I am thankful for the kindness of our pastor, the Reverend Fred Williams, of Snohomish Community Church, who read through this manuscript, checked my theology, and gave valuable suggestions.

INTRODUCTION

Gentle Jesus, meek and mild,
Look upon a little child;
Pity my simplicity,
Suffer me to come to Thee.
     —Charles Wesley

I grew up on lovely Bainbridge Island in Washington State. Our family's white, colonial-style home sat on a bluff overlooking the sparkling blue waters of Puget Sound.

I was number five of six children, and we spent most of our summers on the beach below us. When we stopped swimming and diving from our raft long enough to look, we saw Mount Rainier to the south and Mount Baker to the north, with the snowcapped Cascade Mountains in between. The lights of Seattle glowed like a string of jewels along the distant shore.

Since our beautiful mother, Kathryn, was a professional singer, I didn't know her very well. She kept busy practicing her lessons, singing at weddings or funerals, or darning socks. Maybe I was a bother, for she called me "P-e-s-t" and said I asked too many questions. *Pest* was the first word I knew how to spell.

Our cook and housekeeper, Elizabeth Norton, whom

we called "Nana," created delicious meals, did the laundry, and kept the house immaculate. Mother used to say that Nana ran our place like an institution. She took care of me and let me sleep with her in her big bed. My older siblings teased me and called me "Nana's Pet," but I loved her dearly.

I later learned that my father, Allan Cunningham Sr., emigrated from Scotland in 1903 with his mother, Agnes, and six siblings. After graduating from the University of Washington with an engineering degree, he established the Cunningham Manufacturing Company in Seattle, where he invented and manufactured marine deck machinery. His air whistles "heard round the world" were used on ships, boats, ferries, trains, and lighthouses. Before World War II, he began equipping United States Navy ships.

But I didn't know that my dad was famous in the marine world. To me, he was just a loving father who hugged and kissed me. Later, I learned that I not only bore his mother's name but also looked like her.

If Dad came home on the passenger boat, *Manitou*, instead of the automobile ferry, we kids would run down a long path to meet him at the dock on Yeomalt Point. He would put down his briefcase, hug us, and let us search his pockets for small Hershey bars or gum. As we started back to our house, the older kids would run ahead, stopping long enough to pick and eat huckleberries along the way. But I held onto my daddy's hand and trotted along beside him, just enjoying his presence.

Dad did so many things to show us his love. Early on Easter morning, he filled little woven baskets with colorful eggs and chocolate bunnies and hid them in the garden for us to find when we returned from church.

We often took swimming lessons in the pool at the Washington Athletic Club in Seattle where Dad had a room for his workweek. Then he'd take us to lunch in the elegant dining hall with its white tablecloths and glittering chandeliers.

Christmas was the highlight of the year. While the delicious aromas of turkey and ham floated through the living room, Daddy would read the Christmas story from the Bible to us. Then smiling, he'd reach for the presents under the tree and had my middle brother distribute them.

After I opened my gifts, I would hug Daddy and thank him. My favorite gifts were a Patsy doll in a little red trunk full of doll clothes and a set of Walt Disney china dishes with Three-Little-Pigs designs.

Then with no warning a few months later, my whole world crashed around me. My beloved father went to work one day, caught a bad cold, and was taken to the hospital with pneumonia. Mother rushed to see him, but he was already in a coma by the time she arrived. Since this was before penicillin was discovered, he died four days later at the age of fifty-four.

When Mother returned home and walked in the door, she threw her arms around Nana. Both women wept while we watched and wondered what had happened.

Dave broke the silence when he asked, "How's Dad?"

Mother took out a handkerchief and dried her eyes. "He's gone to heaven," she said softly.

My older siblings seemed to understand and began to cry, but I was so young I didn't have a clue. *Why are they crying?* I wondered. *What's going on? Dad will be back soon, won't he?*

A few days later, relatives drove us to the ferry and into

Seattle to a fancy building. We walked into a big room with lots of people, but our family went behind a curtain and sat there. *Why are we hiding?* I wondered. The people sang hymns quietly, and a couple of men talked. Then folks lined up to walk by a long box in front, and many were crying. Mother and the older kids did too. But as a youngster, I couldn't figure out what was happening.

Afterwards, Mother and we children climbed into a long, black car and headed up a line of cars moving slowly down the street.

Dave didn't know what was going on, either, for he asked Mother, "Where are we going?"

"Shh, dear. It's your father's funeral."

He shook his head. "Can't be. We're going too slow!"

When we arrived at some sort of park, I sat in the big car with Nana while people talked and cried under a big tree.

By the time we reached home, I had decided that Daddy must have gone on another business trip. Surely, he'd be back soon with his warm hugs and his pockets full of chocolate bars and gum.

The next Christmas was different. *Where is Daddy?* I wondered. *His trip must have taken him farther away than usual. And where were the lovely presents? He must not have sent any from his trip.* I got only a couple of coloring books and a box of crayons.

That night it finally dawned on me. After Nana tucked me into bed, I pulled the soft quilt over my face and cried. *Dad really is not coming home—ever! He is gone—the most wonderful person I ever knew, the one who loved me more than anyone else in all the world, the one who hugged and kissed me.* Tears rolled down my cheeks and trickled into my ears. *He must have gone to the place Mother called heaven. Maybe that's where Jesus lives.*

So I prayed silently, "Dear Jesus, if Daddy is with you, please say hi to him for me." I cried and cried with my first pangs of grief until I finally drifted off to sleep.

Later, my dearest friend, Joanne, had an operation and died. Since she was my age, her death shook me to the core. *What will happen to me when I die?* I wondered. This so disturbed me that I finally asked Mother, "If I die, will I go to heaven?"

"You will, if you ask Jesus to be your Savior." She drew me to herself and explained how to do that, then led me in prayer. That was the beginning of my lifetime of following Christ.

For many years, heaven was still a mysterious place to me. I often wondered, *What's it like? Where is it? What does Dad do?* No one ever explained, and I never heard a sermon or a Sunday school lesson about heaven. But as an adult, I searched the Scriptures, and this book is the result of my search.

You might have questions too, because you're human, like me. Maybe you've wondered about the same things— where heaven is, what you'll do there, what you'll look like, who you'll see.

So I wrote this book to tell you one thing—God loves you and has prepared a wonderful home for you in eternity. He knows all your questions. Maybe you have lost your parents, your spouse, a friend. People you love may be deathly ill, and you wish you knew how to comfort them, what Scripture verses to share with them.

You would like to describe heaven to them and tell them what they'll do, who they'll see. You want to assure them that they will have new bodies and that they might even fly through space. And you want to tell them how God often sends his angels to minister to them and angels will finally carry them to heaven.

I hope and pray that this book will answer your questions and draw you closer to Jesus, God's beloved Son. He'll be standing by one of heaven's gates to welcome you with open arms when you arrive.

So read and enjoy learning about the glorious home God has prepared for you. Share this book with others, and get ready to fly!

Here's a poem I wrote indicating my desire to be with Jesus in Glory:

A Love Song to Jesus

Lord, you mean more to me
Than anything on earth can be;
Your glories, much greater far
Than loftiest peak or highest star.

What beauty crowns your fairest brow;
What glory fills your face just now;
Your eyes, so full of love I see
As you hold out your arms to me.

I run, Lord Jesus, to those arms,
A little child, all safe from harm,
To be enfolded to your breast,
To find in you sweet peace and rest.
                           —Agnes C. Lawless

CHAPTER 1
WHAT IS HEAVEN LIKE?

My Father's House is a home prepared especially for you.[1]
—Anne Graham Lotz

A family friend, missionary linguist Dr. Len Newell, spent years on the Philippine island of Luzon learning the unwritten language of the Ifugao people. Then he translated the Bible for these former headhunters.

When Len and his wife left after many years, some one hundred and twenty thousand Ifugao believers had established over one hundred churches.

The Newells retired in Canada where Len developed esophageal cancer, and his wife, Jo, realized that he would soon die. She later told us this account of his passing:

Len was not on pain medications, so his mind was clear. Jo and their adult children gathered around his bed at home, holding his hands, singing hymns, and praying.

Suddenly, Len looked up at the ceiling and said, "Oh, man!"

Jo leaned closer. "What do you see?"

A look of expectation crossed his face. "I see the gates of heaven . . . and Jesus standing, waiting for me . . . and a lot of my family and friends . . . and Ifugao believers are there too!" He began naming them, then his voice grew soft and finally stopped.

With a glowing face still turned upwards, Len took a deep breath, and his spirit slipped into the arms of his Savior in his heavenly home.[2]

Like for Len Newell, our Father God has prepared a glorious place for us in heaven, where he dwells. His Son Jesus lives there too, the one who gave his life for us so we could join him. Thousands upon thousands of angels also dwell in that beautiful place. Moreover, heaven is the home of countless believers, who have gone before us.

Author Henry Bosch writes about a believer, "To that home his whole being aspires, for there is the throne of the God he worships, there is the blessed physical presence of the Christ he adores, and there are the kindred spirits of his loved ones gone before."[3]

Just what is our Father's home like? The Bible only hints about heaven itself, but it provides a detailed description of its capital, the New Jerusalem.

Pastor and author David Jeremiah in his book, *Answers to Questions About Heaven*, suggests that this city "will eventually become the 'capital' of heaven and that final abode of His children."[4]

Heaven Is Glorious

About his vision, the apostle John wrote, "I saw the Holy City, the new Jerusalem, coming down out of heaven from God, prepared as a bride beautifully dressed for her husband" (Revelation 21:2).

Brides always dress as beautifully as possible for their husbands. Even though John and I were rather poor as young missionary candidates, we had fun preparing for our simple wedding. He and a friend cut greenery in the woods to decorate the small church, and we filled baskets with large bouquets of flowers. My bridesmaids made lovely dresses for themselves, and a little flower girl proudly told her friends that she was my "flower pot!"

Since Mother was away, Aunt Beline took me to Frederick and Nelson's, the best department store in Seattle, to buy supplies for the wedding gown we made together. After we chose shimmering satin and intricate lace material, my auntie took me to her dressmaker, who guided our simple V-neck, A-line creation. With a borrowed veil and my aunt's gift of a double string of genuine pearls that sparkled in the candlelight, I felt beautifully dressed for the happy occasion.

But only God can make the holy city more beautiful than a bride dressed in her finery. Every detail is exquisitely crafted. It shines "with the glory of God, and its brilliance was like that of a very precious jewel, like a jasper, clear as crystal" (v. 11).

The heavenly wedding of Jesus and his Bride in the holy city will be lit, not with candles, not with lamps but with the glory of God himself. Scripture says that "the glory of God gives it light, and the Lamb [Jesus] is its lamp" (v. 23).

Heaven Is Huge

Heaven's capital is gigantic—"12,000 stadia" (about 1,400 miles or 2,200 kilometers) in length, "and as wide and high as it is long" (vv. 15–16).

Author Randy Alcorn in his book *Heaven* says, "A metropolis of this size in the middle of the United States would stretch from Canada to Mexico and from the

Appalachian Mountains to the California border."[5] Even more amazing, he suggests it is as high as it is long, so it would tower 1,400 miles into the stratosphere and may be more like a pyramid than a cube. Alcorn also thinks that the ground-level area is nearly two million square miles. We need not fear overcrowding, for it has room for billions of people.[6]

David Jeremiah adds, "Given that this city is cubical, we can assume that it will have more than one level. Remember, we cannot fathom the grandeur of this place. It will be unlike anything we have ever seen, and there is no question that it will be able to house every believer who has ever lived."[7]

When writing the book of Revelation, the apostle John used many references to the Old Testament and often employed symbolic language. In the original Greek, every measurement of the New Jerusalem is a multiple of the number *twelve*.

To the Eastern mind, twelve has always been a number of perfection or completion. Israel had twelve tribes, and Jesus had twelve disciples, so the implication of the word *twelve* is that the New Jerusalem is a perfect size, large enough to accommodate with ease all those who will reside there.

Heaven Is Studded with Jewels

When my cousin, Gail, and I toured England and Scotland some years ago, we went to the Tower of London to see the crown jewels of the United Kingdom. We gazed with awe at the gorgeous display of 140 royal ceremonial crowns and other objects decorated with a total of 23,578 sparkling gems.

But although these jewels are fit only for royalty, Jesus

is preparing a far greater array of dazzling riches for us in the New Jerusalem—a sparkling wall, jewel-studded foundations, gates of pearl, and golden streets.

If we approach heaven from afar, the first object we see will be a shining wall. The apostle John said that an angel measured the New Jerusalem's wall, "and it was 144 cubits [200 feet or 65 meters] thick" (Revelation 21:17). The wall is made of jasper. Since the Bible describes heavenly jasper as "clear as crystal" (v. 11), we may assume that the wall may be translucent.

Then we'll notice the sparkling foundations. John explained that "the wall of the city had twelve foundations, and on them were the names of the twelve apostles of the Lamb" (Revelation 21:14). A different precious stone decorates each foundation. "The first foundation was jasper, the second sapphire, the third agate, the fourth emerald, the fifth onyx, the sixth ruby, the seventh chrysolite, the eighth beryl, the ninth topaz, the tenth turquoise, the eleventh jacinth, and the twelfth amethyst" (vv. 19–20).

Professor and author John F. Walvoord in his commentary, *The Revelation of Jesus Christ*, acknowledges that the precise colors of these stones are uncertain. But, he writes, "The light of the city within shining through these various colors in the foundation of the wall topped by the wall itself composed of the crystal-clear jasper forms a scene of dazzling beauty in keeping with the glory of God and the beauty of His holiness."[8]

Heaven Has Pearly Gates

In his vision, John saw "a great, high wall with twelve gates, and with twelve angels at the gates. On the gates were written the names of the twelve tribes of Israel"

(Revelation 21:12). The great wall has three gates on the east, three on the west, three on the north, and three on the south (v. 13). John also saw that each gate was made of a single pearl (v. 21).

Heaven Has Golden Streets

Two materials used in building heaven's capital city were gold and precious stones. John said, "The great street of the city was of gold, as pure as transparent glass" (Revelation 21:21), and precious stones decorate the foundation (vv. 19–20).

Throughout history, builders have always used available and easily acquired materials. By using such words as *gold* and *precious stones*, the Bible suggests that items we value on earth are of common use in heaven.

Archeologists discovered King Tutankhamen's tomb in Egypt in 1922 and unearthed amazing treasures made of solid gold—a coffin, a facemask, boxes, chests, and jewelry. But nothing of King Tut compares with the glorious treasures of heaven.

Heaven Has Beautiful Housing

We may wonder what kind of housing we will have in heaven. Jesus told his disciples, "My Father's house has many rooms; if that were not so, would I have told you that I am going there to prepare a place for you?" (John 14:2). We don't know what type of structures we will live in, but I'm sure they will be beautiful.

Pastor and author Don Baker in his book, *Heaven: A Glimpse of Your Future Home*, writes: "I'm not sure whether our place is going to be a single-family residence, a condominium, a town house, an apartment, or something altogether different. I am certain, however, that it will be something far superior to anything anyone has ever known here on earth, and all this without maintenance, or upkeep."[9]

Heaven Has a Crystal River

John described the heavenly landscaping. He saw "the river of the water of life, as clear as crystal, flowing from the throne of God and of the Lamb down the middle of the great street of the city" (Revelation 22:1–2). On each side of the river stands the tree of life, "bearing twelve crops of fruit, yielding its fruit every month," and the leaves are for the "healing of the nations" (v. 2).

Professor and author Merrill C. Tenney suggests that the term "tree of life" is collective, so perhaps entire rows of trees grow along the river. The city may also be full of beautiful parks.[10]

Just Think

Our Father's heavenly home is glorious, huge, and sparkling with jewels. It has a shining wall, jewel-studded foundations, pearly gates, golden streets, beautiful housing, and a crystal-clear river surrounded by parks.

Since Jesus has prepared a glorious home for you, you can be assured that he and your friends will be standing at a pearly gate, waiting to welcome you with open arms when you arrive.

I Heard a Sound of Voices

I saw the holy city,
The New Jerusalem,
Come down from Heav'n, a bride adorned

With jeweled diadem;
The flood of crystal waters
Flowed down the golden street;
And nations brought their honors there
And laid them at her feet.

And there no sun was needed,
Nor moon to shine by night,
God's glory did enlighten all,
The Lamb Himself the Light;
And there His servants serve Him,
And, life's long battle o'er,
Enthroned with Him, their Savior King,
They reign forevermore.

—Godfrey Thring (1823–1903)

CHAPTER 2

WHAT WILL WE BE LIKE IN HEAVEN?

We're going to have real bodies—physical, transformed bodies like the body of the Lord Jesus when He was resurrected from the grave.[1]

—David Jeremiah

"Want to sparkle?" a newspaper advertisement asks. It suggests relighting your inner flame with facials, skin-care treatments, and detoxifying body wraps. Another ad touts laser-based procedures: "Look years younger without surgery. Experience the light!" Cosmetic clinics promise to fix everything from sagging eyelids and excess fat to wrinkles and varicose veins.

On a popular TV program, the hosts choose a contestant, dump her old wardrobe in a garbage can, give her fashion advice, and buy her new outfits. Then they send her to a salon for a professional hairstyle and makeup to complete her extreme makeover.

We live in a day of makeovers on and off television, but someday each of us will receive an extreme makeover in heaven. What will that involve?

Christ's resurrected body hints at the changes we can

expect, for the Bible tells us "we shall be like him" (1 John 3:2). In fact, he "will transform our lowly bodies so that they will be like his glorious body" (Philippians 3:21). So what was Jesus like after his resurrection? And what will we be like?

We'll Have Extreme Makeovers

Jesus's appearance must have changed after his resurrection. Since the Roman soldiers had taken his clothes at his crucifixion, he obviously wore something different afterwards. That may have been one reason why his friends and disciples did not recognize him at first. His bodily features may have changed somewhat too.

For instance, when Mary Magdalene went to his tomb, an angel told her that Jesus had risen from the dead. She looked around, saw a man standing in the garden, and assumed he was the gardener. But when he said, " 'Mary,' she turned toward him and cried out in Aramaic, 'Rabboni!' (which means Teacher)" (John 20:16).

That same day, two of his followers walking to the village of Emmaus discussed Jesus's crucifixion and the rumors of his resurrection.

Jesus joined them and explained Old Testament prophecies about the Messiah, "but they were kept from recognizing him" (Luke 24:16). When they reached Emmaus, Jesus acted as if he were going to walk on, but they urged him to stay for supper. Around the table, Jesus played the part of the host, saying the blessing, breaking a loaf of bread, and passing it to them in his old manner. It may have been when they saw the nail scars on his hands that instantly "their eyes were opened and they recognized him, and he disappeared from their sight" (v. 31).

Later, Jesus walked through a closed door to join his disciples. Startled and frightened, they thought he was a ghost. He said, "Why are you troubled, and why do doubts rise in your minds? Look at my hands and my feet. It is I myself!" (Luke 24:38–39).

Still later, several disciples fished all night in the Sea of Galilee but caught nothing. Early in the morning, they saw a man standing on the shore but did not recognize him.

He called out, "Friends, haven't you any fish?" When they answered no, he said, "Throw your net on the right side of the boat and you will find some" (John 21:5–6).

They did and caught so many fish that they were unable to haul in the net. Only then did John say, "It is the Lord!" (v. 7).

When the disciples landed their vessel, they saw a fire of coals with fish and bread toasting. Jesus said, "Come and have breakfast" (v. 12).

Scripture says, "None of the disciples dared ask him, 'Who are you?' They knew it was the Lord" (v. 12).

Author David Winter says, "It was the miracle he had done and the personality they knew so well that convinced them that they were once again in the presence of their Lord."[2]

Because we will be like Christ, our resurrected bodies will look different from our earthly ones. Paul says the body is like a planted seed that changes when it emerges from the ground: "The body that is sown is perishable, it is raised imperishable; it is sown in dishonor, it is raised in glory; it is sown in weakness, it is raised in power; it is sown a natural body, it is raised a spiritual body" (1 Corinthians 15:42–44).

Paul explains further, "Just as we have borne the image of the earthly man, so shall we bear the image of the heavenly man" (v. 49).

In fact, when Christ comes to take believers to himself, "we will all be changed—in a flash, in the twinkling of an eye, at the last trumpet. For the trumpet will sound, the dead will be raised imperishable, and we will be changed. For the perishable must clothe itself with the imperishable, and the mortal with immortality" (1 Corinthians 15:51–53).

Pastor and author David Jeremiah says, "Our bodies are in the graves until the resurrection at the rapture when the trumpet sounds. Then our bodies will be transformed into our permanent, heavenly bodies."[3]

Years ago, a tall young man knocked on our door. When I answered, he said, "You may not remember me, but you were my first-grade teacher." As he sat down and told me about himself, I looked him over. Yes, this was Robby with the same features, but now he was a handsome young man instead of a little boy.

Perhaps this is a dim picture of how we'll be changed when we get to heaven. We'll look similar to how we appear now—only better!

We'll Wear New Clothes

Like Jesus, we'll wear new clothes in heaven. The apostle John says, "The wedding of the Lamb has come, and his bride has made herself ready. Fine linen, bright and clean, was given her to wear" (Revelation 19:7–8). Although the "bride" refers to the Church composed of all believers, the linen given to her may also refer to the white clothes we'll apparently wear as individuals.

When a bride prepares for her wedding, she not only buys or borrows a beautiful white gown for the occasion, but she also buys other lovely outfits if possible. This often is a time when her mother, sister, or friends have an exiting time shopping with her. It's all part of the bride making herself ready for her beloved.

Even so, as the Bride of Christ, we'll be given glorious new clothes to spend eternity with him.

We'll Have Flesh and Bones

When Jesus came through the closed door to his disciples and they thought he was a ghost, he said, "Touch me and see; a ghost does not have flesh and bones, as you see I have" (Luke 24:39).

Thomas, who joined the other disciples a week later, refused to believe that Jesus was alive. He said, "Unless I see the nail marks in his hands and put my finger where the nails were, and put my hands into his side, I will not believe" (John 20:25).

But Jesus convinced him by allowing the doubter to touch the scars in his hands and side. Jesus said, "Stop doubting and believe" (v. 27).

Thomas's response was, "My Lord and my God!" (v. 28).

Apparently, we too will have flesh and bones in our glorified bodies.

We'll Be Able to Eat

Jesus showed his frightened disciples that he was a real person by asking, " 'Do you have anything here to eat?' They gave him a piece of broiled fish, and he took it and ate it in their presence" (Luke 24:41–43).

The book of Revelation speaks of a great banquet Christ is preparing for believers, his bride—the "wedding supper of the Lamb" (Revelation 19:9). We'll be able to eat and enjoy doing so.

Weddings usually involve food and drink. John and I

were married in the days when the bride's family provided simple refreshments, such as cake, ice cream, pink and green peppermints, and drinks.

But things are different now. At a recent wedding Dan and attended, the bride's family provided the two hundred guests with a delicious meal—fruit salad, Parmesan chicken, roasted potatoes, green beans in a special sauce, fresh rolls, wedding cake with ice cream, as well as sparkling cider, tea, and coffee.

At the wedding supper of the Lamb, we'll have a more elegant meal than we can imagine. I can't even suggest the menu. But it will be a glorious, happy occasion with our Bridegroom, the King of kings and Lord of lords.

We Can Travel Through Space

On the first evening after Jesus's resurrection "when the disciples were together, with the doors locked for fear of the Jewish leaders, Jesus came and stood among them" (John 20:19). A week later, the disciples were in the house again, and Thomas was with them. "Though the doors were locked, Jesus came and stood among them and said, 'Peace be with you!'" (v. 26).

Without using ordinary means, Jesus apparently "space traveled" from talking with Mary in the garden, to the men walking to Emmaus, to the disciples behind closed doors, to breakfast on the shores of Galilee, to the Mount of Ascension—all many miles apart. On the last occasion, his followers "looked intently up into the sky as he was going" until a cloud obscured their view (Acts 1:9–10).

Author Randy Alcorn in his book *In Light of Eternity* says that Christ's ascension to heaven suggests that with our new bodies, "we may be able to fly and transcend the present laws of physics."[4]

When we were children, my brother Dave built a platform in our huge maple tree, hung a thick rope on a branch, and jumped off, swinging through space and using his "Tarzan of the Apes" call.

But things had changed by the time that John's and my son, Kenny, was a year old during Apollo 11's landing in space. Just as astronaut Neil Armstrong took his first step on the moon, our son took his first step on earth. I got more excited over that than the moonwalk! Now NASA plans to shoot a spacecraft that could send high-definition videos from Mars to earth, using laser beams.

However, such advanced technology will seem as nothing when we get to heaven. Author and pastor Don Baker thinks our bodies "will be designed for a new dimension." They will "not be limited by space and time, and, like Jesus' body, will pass through matter and probably move through space with the speed of thought."[5]

Just Think

In heaven, we'll have perfect bodies that have flesh and bones, we'll be dressed in spotless white clothes, we will eat with Jesus and others, we can walk through doors, and we can travel through space. What glorious makeovers!

Soon Shall the Trump of God
Soon shall the trump of God
Give out the welcome sound
That shakes death's silent chamber walls
And breaks the turf-sealed ground.
You dwellers in the dust

Awake, come forth, and sing;
Sharp has your frost of winter been,
But bright shall be your spring.

'Twas sown in weakness here;
'Twill then be raised in power;
That which was sown an earthly seed
Shall rise a heav'nly flower.

—Horatius Bonar, 1857 (1808–1889)

CHAPTER 3

WHERE IS HEAVEN?

*It does not matter what part of the globe we may stand
upon; heaven is above us.*[1]

—D. L. Moody

When I was young, I knew that five women—Elizabeth
Norton ("Nana"), Mandy Berg, Emma Curtis, Mrs. Green,
and Mother—met once a week for prayer. But I didn't know
that they were praying especially for three unconverted
husbands—Richard Curtis, Al Berg, and Dad.

Mother and Nana told me later that they prayed
earnestly for several years, even when the men either made
fun of or ignored their beliefs. But before they died, all
three men had accepted Christ as Savior and Lord of their
lives.

Our neighbor, Richard Curtis, was the first to do so.
He had seen no need for church—or Christianity, for that
matter. He had let his wife attend to such things. But he
was a fine man, an upstanding citizen, and his life revolved
around his chicken farm.

His wife, Emma, a former teacher and a radiant
Christian, studied her Bible, taught the adult class in
our Sunday school, and prayed earnestly for her husband.

Eventually, she had the joy of leading Richard to the Lord. Then he contracted a fatal illness, and doctors gave him no hope of recovery.

One Sunday, Louise, a family friend, volunteered to stay with him so Emma could attend church. As Louise was peeling potatoes for dinner, she heard Richard call and went to his room.

"Do you have the radio on?" he asked.

"No, I don't."

"But I'm hearing the most beautiful music!" With a wide smile, he sat up in bed as he gazed earnestly toward the ceiling. Then he fell back lifeless onto the pillows.

He had been ushered *up* into heaven.

But before we talk about heaven's location, let's establish the fact that it is an actual reality.

Heaven Is a Real Place

Many believers don't seem to know much about our final destination, although the Bible contains over six hundred references to heaven. In his book, *Answers to Your Questions About Heaven*, pastor and author David Jeremiah declares that "heaven is a literal place prepared by Christ for a prepared people."[2]

Author and former pastor Charles Swindoll agrees. In his book *Growing Deep in the Christian Life*, he wrote, "It is very important that you understand heaven, our eternal destiny, is an *actual place*. It isn't a misty dream or a floating fantasy. Don't let any of the mystical religions confuse you. Heaven is reality. Literal real estate, which He is preparing for His own."[3]

Author, former college president, and pastor James T. Jeremiah (David Jeremiah's father) wrote, "Heaven is a real place, much more than the 'beautiful isle of somewhere' described by the poet. Before Jesus went to the cross, He promised, 'I go to prepare a *place* for you' (John 14:2 KJV). The dictionary defines a *place* as a 'definite location.'"[4]

Heaven Has Various Names

Biblical authors use various names or terms for heaven. They call it:

"a city" (Hebrews 11:10)

"a country" (Hebrews 11:14)

"the Father's house" (John 14:2)

"the eternal kingdom" (2 Peter 1:11)

"the paradise of God" (Revelation 2:7)

"a place" (John 14:3)

Heaven not only has various names, but the name *heaven* refers to different sections.

Three Heavens

We see the first heaven in the daytime, the second in the nighttime, and we see the third heaven by faith in the Scriptures.

The apostle Paul said that one day he was "caught up to the third heaven" (2 Corinthians 12:2). So a third heaven implies that there must be a first and second heaven also.

The First Heaven

The first heaven is the area immediately above us. During the creation, God called this expanse "sky" (Genesis 1:8). It contains puffy white clouds that decorate blue skies in nice weather and dark clouds, which yield rain, hail, and snow.

The first heaven is also the area where birds fly, those wonderful creatures of God's creation. We live in an area of Washington State where several thousands of trumpeter swans fly down from British Columbia to spend the winter. These majestic white birds have black beaks and wingspans of up to ten feet. Since they spend nights in ponds along the Snohomish River near us, we watch them fly past our home in v-shaped groups, trumpeting loudly as they're off to spend the day nibbling in harvested cornfields.

One day I was walking along our road when a flock of trumpeters flew right over my head. Amazed, I could hear their great feathers swishing together.

The Second Heaven

The sun, moon, stars, and planets whirl in the stellar space of the second heaven. On the third day of creation, God "made two great lights"—the sun and the moon and decorated the night sky with stars (Genesis 1:16).

The psalmist was amazed at this display of God's greatness when he wrote, "When I consider your heavens, the work of your fingers, the moon and the stars, which you have set in place, what is mankind that you are mindful of them, human beings that you care for them?" (Psalm 8:3–4).

Pastor and author Don Baker writes in his book, *Heaven: A Glimpse of Your Future Home*, about the "thousand million galaxies in our universe" and the "150 million, million, million stars, of which only two thousand can be seen by the naked eye on a clear night."[5]

When my husband, John, and I were in the Philippines, just seven degrees from the equator, we marveled at the stars in the southern hemisphere. We often took the missionary kids up on a hill at night, where they flopped down on woven mats and took turns looking through John's telescope at the amazing constellations. I wonder if the children, now grown adults, remember those heart-warming times.

The Third Heaven

The triune God, his angels, and believers who have gone before inhabit the third heaven.

Author and teacher John R. Rice said, "For the Christian, Heaven will be where Christ is. He is now there with the Father. But one day He will come and receive us and take us away to those heavenly mansions."[6]

When Jesus was comforting his disciples before his death, he said, "My Father's house has many rooms; if that were not so, would I have told you that I am going there to prepare a place for you?" (John 14:2).

To assure them that they would be with him, Jesus added, "And if I go and prepare a place for you, I will come back and take you to be with me that you also may be with me where I am" (v. 3).

So wherever Jesus is, that will be heaven.

But do we have any indication of just where the third heaven is located?

Heaven Is Above Us

Evangelist D. L. Moody said that soon after he was converted, an infidel asked him why he looked up when he prayed. The scoffer claimed that heaven was "no more above us than below us; that heaven was everywhere."[7]

But when Moody knew his Bible better, he realized that "heaven is above, God is in heaven, and heaven is above our heads."[8]

David Jeremiah agrees that we do not know where heaven is precisely, but "we know that it is up."[9] In fact, he says that the Old Testament Hebrew word for heaven is *shamayim,* which means "the heights." The New Testament Greek word, *ouranos,* means "raised up or lofty."[10]

The prophet Isaiah declared that God lives up in "a high and holy place" (Isaiah 57:15). The prophet Jeremiah urged, "Let us lift up our hearts and our hands to God in heaven" (Lamentations 3:41).

The apostle Paul wrote, "For the Lord himself will come down from heaven, with a loud command, with the voice of the archangel and with the trumpet call of God, and the dead in Christ will rise first. After that, we who are still alive and are left will be caught up together with them in the clouds to meet the Lord in the air. And so we will be with the Lord forever" (1 Thessalonians 4:16–17).

After Jesus rose from the dead, he taught his disciples for forty days. He gave them his final words then he "was taken up before their very eyes, and a cloud hid him from their sight" (Acts 1:9).

His followers "were looking intently up into the sky as he was going, when suddenly two angels dressed in white stood beside them. 'Men of Galilee,' they said, 'why do you stand here looking into the sky?'" (vv. 10–11). They assured the disciples that Jesus would come back in the same way they had seen him go up into heaven (v. 11).

During the early days of the church, Jewish leaders dragged the apostle Stephen before their council with false accusations. Stephen preached a powerful sermon about their unbelief, and they became enraged. Just before they stoned him to death, Stephen "looked up to heaven and saw the glory of God, and Jesus standing at the right hand of God" (Acts 7:55).

When God considers his people, he looks down. Moses

prayed, "Look down from heaven, your holy dwelling place, and bless your people" (Deuteronomy 26:15).

In a vision, the apostle John said that he "saw the Holy City, the new Jerusalem, coming down "out of heaven from God" (Revelation 21:2).

Could Heaven Be in the North?

Years ago, one of my teachers gave an interesting talk in chapel about the possible location of heaven. He based his theory on God saying that he stretches "out the north over the empty place" (Job 26:7 KJV); that Zion is "on the sides of the north" (Psalm 48:2); and that Lucifer wanted to sit above the stars on "the sides of the north" (Isaiah 14:13).

I never forgot this teacher's talk and often wondered if heaven could be located in the "empty place" in the "sides of the north." But most Bible study notes discount this idea. For instance, *The MacArthur Study Bible*, using the NKJV, has this translation of Psalm 48:2, much like the old KJV: "Beautiful in elevation, the joy of the whole earth, is Mount Zion on the sides of the north, the city of the great King." However, a note explains that "north" here refers to Zaphon, an "ancient Near Eastern equivalent to Mt. Olympus, the dwelling place of pagan gods."[11]

The NIV Study Bible agrees, adding that "Mount Zaphon in the far north was for the Phoenicians the sacred residence of El, the chief of their gods."[12]

The Ryrie Study Bible (NAS) simply says that the far north in heathen lore was the "abode of the gods."[13]

Now, however, since larger and more powerful telescopes are making new discoveries in the skies, some Bible teachers and theologians may be changing their tunes.

For instance, David Jeremiah, in his book, *Revealing*

the Mysteries of Heaven, refers to the phrase in Isaiah 14:13 of the "farthest sides of the north." He tells about the 2015 report of astronomers in Hawaii who have discovered a huge hole in the universe—1.8 billion light years across. He writes:

> No matter where you are on earth, north will always be up. So it would seem reasonable to conclude that heaven is somewhere in the northern universe beyond the reach of the astronomers' telescopes. And when I read scientists' reports that a place exists in the northern heavens that seems strangely vacant of stars and galaxies, it validates that conclusion.[14]

I came across something similar on *Space.com* in an article titled, "Huge Hole Found in the Universe":

> The universe has a huge hole in it that dwarfs anything else of its kind. The discovery caught astronomers by surprise. The hole is nearly a billion in light years across. It is not a black hole . . . Rather, this one is mostly devoid of stars, gas, and other normal matter, and it's also strangely empty of the mysterious 'dark matter' that permeates the cosmos. Other space voids have been found before, but nothing on this scale.[15]

Researcher Lawrence Rudnick of the University of Minnesota adds, "Not only has no one ever found a void this big, but we never even expected to find one this size."[16] Astronomers say they made this discovery by using the Very Large Array (VLA) radio telescope, funded by the National Science Foundation.[17]

So perhaps it is safe to conclude that the abode of God is in the third heaven, that it is above us, and that it might be in an empty space in the northern area of the universe.

Whatever, we believers will be going home, and we should be getting excited. This reminds me about our little cockapoo, Blackie. If we went out of town, we always returned the same way. She would be sound asleep, but when we turned *a certain corner*, she woke up immediately, scrambled to an open window, and stuck her head out. Then she would bark and whine the rest of the way. She was going home!

Have you turned *a certain corner* in your life where the journey to heaven seems closer, maybe just up the road? Perhaps you're dealing with a fatal disease, or you are the caregiver for someone who is. Or maybe your loving spouse just died . . . or a child . . . or a parent, and you are overwhelmed with grief. The tears flow so easily and so often. You wonder if you can ever come up for air. I know. I've been there.

Just Think

Heaven is a real place. This abode of God is located in the third heaven above us, and it may be in an empty space in the northern part of the universe.

So let's get excited—for we're on our way HOME, and how wonderful our arrival will be!

JUST THINK—
Of stepping on shore and finding it Heaven;
Of taking hold of a hand and finding it God's hand;
Of breathing a new air and finding it celestial air;

Of feeling invigorated and finding it immortality;
Of passing from storm and tempest to an unbroken calm;
Of looking up—and finding it HOME!
                              —Author unknown

When the Roll Is Called Up Yonder
When the trumpet of the Lord shall sound,
And time shall be no more,
And the morning breaks, eternal, bright and fair;
When the saved of earth shall gather
Over on the other shore,
And the roll is called up yonder, I'll be there.

On that bright and cloudless morning
When the dead in Christ shall rise,
And the glory of his resurrection share;
When his chosen ones shall gather
To their home beyond the skies,
And the roll is called up yonder, I'll be there.
                    —James Milton Black (1856–1938)

Chapter 4
What Is Not in Heaven?

Soon we pass this desert dreary,
Soon we bid farewell to pain;
Never more are sad or weary,
Never, never sin again.
—Horatius Bonar

As baby number five, I was so small that the doctor told Mother that she would never raise me. When she quit nursing me, I was too frail to drink out of a bottle or to eat baby food. So she fed me milk with a tiny spoon. This exasperated her, and one day she said outloud, "What am I going to do with this child?"

Dubbed "Nana" by the older children, our cook and housekeeper, Elizabeth Norton, said, "Give her to me." She cuddled me, cooed to me, and fed me with great delight, no matter how long it took. She even wheeled my crib into her bedroom, and from then on, I slept near her or with her until I was older. I became her darling child, and we loved each other dearly. Years later, she put her arms around me and told me that she had saved my life with her care.

She had a reason for this love. When Elizabeth worked in Alaska as a young woman, she married a soldier, Robert

Norton. Then World War I broke out, and the US Army shipped him to France, leaving her with baby son, Bobby. Her husband returned to the States after the war but wrote her a "Dear John" letter, saying he had fallen in love with someone else, and he asked for a divorce. That was almost unheard of in those days, so Elizabeth was devastated.

Little Bobby, with his golden curls and sunny ways, had been born deaf. At four years of age, he accompanied his mother one day when she shopped in downtown Seattle. Standing on a corner, he pulled away from her grasp and ran into the street to see something interesting.

But Bobby couldn't hear a streetcar rattling towards him with its clanging bell and screeching brakes. Just as the young mother dashed out to save him, the streetcar crushed him. Her heart was as broken as his little body.

Although I was a functional substitute for Bobby, Nana never fully recovered. I used to wonder why she often cried at night. When she would take me with her to Seattle, we went to Mount Pleasant Cemetery to plant a geranium and trim the grass on Bobby's grave. I could always find his stone when I ran ahead, because a little lamb decorated the top.

When she was in her eighties, Nana wept as she told me, "No one knows what I've suffered from Bobby's loss." Now in heaven, she has undoubtedly found him again with great delight. Her sorrow and tears are gone.

Heaven Has No Tears or Sorrow

After my husband, John, died from cancer, I cried almost every day for months. We had been married for many years, so I missed him sorely. I couldn't seem to stop the tears during my daily quiet time with the Lord. But his Word comforted me, especially the psalms. The good part of that experience is that now I can understand the pain other people experience when they lose their spouses.

For instance, a dear friend lost his spouse after a long illness. One evening he appeared at our door. "I need prayer," he said.

We invited him in, and he sat on a comfortable chair. When I noticed that he was shivering, I brought in a cup of hot coffee to warm him up.

Between sips, the tears flowed. As he wiped them away with a big handkerchief, he told us details about his wife's illness and death. Then he added, "Not many understand. Some are telling me to quit grieving and to get on with my life. But I can't do that yet."

Dan and I said that we understood, having lost our own spouses. Then we prayed for God to comfort and strengthen him. Finally, we reminded him that in heaven God will wipe away our tears, take away our sorrows, and give us joy.

Jesus told about a rich man who lived in luxury and a beggar named Lazarus, who camped outside the rich man's gate. When they both died, the angels carried Lazarus to Abraham's side, but the rich man went to hades. In fiery torment, he begged Abraham to send Lazarus with a dripping wet finger to touch his tongue and relieve his agony.

But Abraham refused, saying, "Son, remember that in your lifetime you received your good things, while Lazarus received bad things, but now he is comforted here and you are in agony" (Luke 16:25).

In the same way, God will comfort us in heaven. The prophet Isaiah said, "The Sovereign Lord will wipe away the tears from all faces" (Isaiah 25:8). The psalmist wrote, "Weeping may stay for the night, but rejoicing comes in the morning" (Psalm 30:5).

Author and pastor E. M. Bounds in his book, *A Place Called Heaven,* says, "No tears are there to flood your heart, no sorrows there to break it, no losses there to grieve and embitter it."[1]

No Abandonments or Rejections

When I was a young teenager, my mother decided to go overseas to do missionary work. When I asked why she was going, she said, "Oh, you don't need me anymore."

But I did. She put my younger brother and me in school dormitories, and off she went, leaving us penniless and homeless. Our older siblings had gone on to other things, so our family had been torn apart. I not only felt abandoned, but I also felt rejected.

Later, memories flooded back, and I wrote this for a college class:

Painful Memories
A stone o'erturned,
Thoughts scurry to find
New recesses
Of the mind.
—Agnes C. Lawless

Mother was gone for ten years without coming back. Upon her return, I felt as if I didn't know her, and our relationship was strained.

The best part is that my experience has given me a heart for others who have gone through similar times. As an adult, I met a young woman whose parents, missionaries in Africa, sent her to the States alone for her high school and college years, and she had to fend for herself. They came back once during that time, but she too felt as if she didn't know them, and their relationship was strained.

But in heaven, those dark clouds will all be gone.

Heaven Has No Curse

When my brothers and I were in college, our aunt often invited us for dinner. We took the bus to our uncle's office in Seattle and rode to their home in his sleek silver Packard. When we arrived, our aunt always encouraged us to walk through their garden while we waited for the meal. On their hillside overlooking Lake Washington, gorgeous roses and other flowers made a spectacular display.

After Adam and Eve sinned, God placed a curse on the earth. The curse included pain in childbirth (Genesis 3:16), thorns and weeds in the ground, and hard work to produce food (vss. 17–19). From then on, "the whole creation has been groaning as in the pains of childbirth right up to the present time" (Romans 8:22). Plants, animals, and people are all under this curse. But in heaven and the New Jerusalem, the Bible says, "No longer will there be any curse" (Revelation 22:3).

Author and professor Merrill Tenney explains, "Not labor, but grueling, fruitless toil is a curse . . . The work in [the city of God] will be delightful service."[2]

Heaven Has No Death

One Saturday morning, a nurse from my aunt's retirement home called and said that Auntie had fallen and should go to the hospital.

When John and I drove her there, a doctor decided that

this ninety-four-year old should stay a while so they could examine her more closely.

The next day when I visited, she was sitting up knitting an afghan. We chatted, and she smiled. "Everything is all right between the Lord and me," she said. "I've just been quoting Psalm 23, which I learned at my mother's knee."

I hugged her. "I love you," I said with tears.

The following day, we learned that she had passed away peacefully in the night. The Lord had assured her of his presence through his Word, so death held no fears for her.

We never know when death may strike, and the fear of it haunts many. But for believers, God's words regarding heaven should encourage us: "There will be no more death or mourning" (Revelation 21:4).

Paul says that at Christ's second coming, "the dead will be raised imperishable, and we will be changed . . . Then the saying that is written will come true: 'Death has been swallowed up in victory'" (1 Corinthians 15:52, 54).

My college English professor wrote this poem about the death of a loved one. Since it's rather long, here's just part of it:

From Death to Birth
Strange.
Her tired body's final child
Will be herself,
A blithe new resident
For heaven's realms.

It is a death,
Yet her rasping, strident breath,
Too strained for speech,

Is also birth cry,
The beginning
Of all the dazzled hymns
That she will soon be singing, singing,
Over there.

—Elva McAllaster

Heaven Has No Pain or Sickness

Charles Haddon Spurgeon, the "prince of preachers" in the 1800s, regularly preached to London crowds of six thousand people. God's blessing rested on his ministry. He had many converts, his printed sermons and books circulated around the world, and the orphanage and pastors' college he founded prospered.

However, for many years gout, or joint inflammation, caused him severe pain.[3] Spurgeon rejoiced to know that in heaven "there will be no more . . . pain" (Revelation 21:4).

Heaven Has No Sin

After hurricane Katrina hit the Gulf Coast in September 2005, broken levees allowed water to flood New Orleans. The resulting devastation unleashed a wave of criminal behavior— uninhibited looting along with hospital- and nursing-home patients being abandoned, raped, even murdered. This behavior reminded us of humanity's sinful hearts.

The apostle John makes it clear that no sin can enter heaven or the New Jerusalem: "Nothing impure will ever enter it, nor will anyone who does what is shameful or deceitful" (Revelation 21:27).

Author Sam Storms in his magazine article, "Heaven: The Eternal Increase of Joy," wrote:

When we get to heaven, there will be nothing

that is abrasive, irritating, agitating or hurtful. Nothing harmful, hateful, upsetting or unkind. Nothing weak, sick, broken or foolish. Nothing deformed, degenerate, depraved or disgusting. Nothing polluted, pathetic, poor or putrid. Nothing dark, dismal, dismaying or degrading. Nothing blameworthy, blemished, blasphemous or blighted. Nothing grotesque or grievous, hideous or insidious. Nothing illicit or illegal, lascivious or lustful. Nothing marred or mutilated, misaligned or misinformed, soiled or spoiled, vile or vicious.[4]

Heaven Has No Sun, Moon, or Night

Ancient cities used lamps and torches to provide lighting. Not much sunlight penetrated the narrow streets by day nor did much moonlight by night. Danger lurked in the dark alleys. Down through the years to the present time, evil and crime have flourished in darkness.

But the Bible says the New Jerusalem "does not need the sun or the moon to shine on it, for the glory of God gives it light, and the Lamb is its lamp" (Revelation 21:23). Furthermore, "there will be no more night" (22:5).

Someone speculated what part of the world has the longest day. In New York City, the longest day is fifteen hours; in Stockholm, eighteen and a half hours; in Spitzbergen, Norway, three and a half months.[5]

But in the New Jerusalem, a day lasts forever. The city will not need hydroelectric power, nuclear energy, or solar panels to light its streets and buildings. Instead, the glory of God the Father and God the Son will illumine the city and the whole new earth.

Heaven Has No Temples or Churches

When John wrote the book of Revelation, pagan temples filled the cities of the Greco-Roman world, and people offered sacrifices to appease their gods as they prayed for counsel and protection.

In his vision of the New Jerusalem, John noted that "God's dwelling place is now among the people, and he will dwell with them" (Revelation 21:3). That's why he later said that he "did not see a temple in the city, because the Lord God Almighty and the Lamb are its temple" (21:22).

The Westminster Catechism says that this world's sin and misery is a result of the fall of mankind. In heaven all the results of the fall, which we experience daily here on earth, will be deleted.

Late one Saturday night while finishing up a sermon, Pastor Fred Zoeller pressed the wrong computer key and deleted the whole piece he'd been working on. He had to reconstruct the entire text from memory and his notes.

Just Think

Every item of what will not be in heaven is connected to a need—tears and sorrow; abandonment and rejection; earth's curse; death; pain and sickness; sin; sun, moon, and night; and temples or churches.

But in heaven we'll have joy, acceptance, abundant life, excellent health, endless light, and we'll worship the King of kings and the Lord of lords throughout all ages.

Can This Be Death?

Can this be death—
To be released from fear and sorrow,
From sickness, weariness and pain?

To be removed from sin's enslavement,
From Satan's influence and domain?

Can this be death—
To be presented in His presence,
The One who loves me evermore?
To be accepted in the fullness
Of Christ, whom I adore?

Can this be death—
To know complete fulfillment
As I look upon His face?
To feast upon the glories
And the riches of His grace?

No, this is Life—
With all that it can offer,
It is joy that overflows!
It is peace that knows no measure,
It is victory o'er my foes!

     —Author unknown

No Night There

In the land of fadeless day
Lies the city foursquare;
It shall never pass away,
And there is no night there.

God shall wipe away all tears,
There's no death, no pain, nor fears,
And they count not time by years,
For there is no night there.

     —John R. Clements

CHAPTER 5

WHAT WILL WE DO IN HEAVEN?

Actually, in Heaven we are going to do some of the same things we do here on earth.[1]

—Don Baker

My husband, Dan Weaver, grew up in Lancaster County, Pennsylvania, and the strong American work ethic influenced him. His father, a wholesale florist, raised flowers and sold them to shops in Pittsburgh and Philadelphia.

Mr. Weaver taught his nine children to work along with him in his greenhouses, where they planted, weeded, and grew his specialties—large chrysanthemums and sweet peas. When it was time to harvest the blooms, he and the family worked quickly to pick and pack them in cardboard boxes for shipping.

Dan's father served his Lord, his customers, and his family well. Even though he had to leave school in the sixth grade to help his parents, he put all nine of his own children through college with his "flower power." To Dan, his father was the symbol of a true servant.

In our heavenly home, we will not only serve God, but

we will also worship him, fellowship with others, learn more, administer with Jesus, and rest from our earthly labors.

We Will Serve God

My first husband, John, was the ultimate handyman. No problem seemed too great for him to tackle. After he retired from teaching, he joined volunteers from our church to help widows, single ladies, or women with non-handy husbands. He repaired cars, fixed clocks, built fences, hung pictures, took discards to Goodwill or the dump, arranged yard sales, and helped people move. They soon proclaimed that John "could do anything!"

He came from a long line of handy people, his mother among them. She kept a box of tools under her kitchen sink and could fix most household problems. Because she lived across the country from us, John called her often as she aged and asked what she was doing. One time she said she had climbed an apple tree to prune it. Another time she had used a ladder and cleaned out the gutters on her two-storied house—all this when she was in her 80s. She's now in heaven, but she's no doubt pruning the heavenly roses or looking for screws to tighten.

When the Bible says that we will serve our Lord in heaven, I imagine that he will give us creative work that will suit our talents and interests. Pastor and author David Jeremiah agrees and wrote, "God has a great plan for each one of us to be wonderfully, happily, excitedly employed—serving the Lord in Paradise. And we will be serving in the fullest expression of the capacity God has given us and using the giftedness He has placed within us."[2]

We may not work in God's gardens, but our activities will be special. Author and educator James T. Jeremiah

(David Jeremiah's father) wrote: "Precisely what work we will do, what ministry of love, what errands for the Lord we will run or what studies we will pursue, not one of us can know as yet. But you can be sure Heaven is not a place of idleness."[3]

God ordained that people work here on earth. He put Adam in the Garden of Eden "to work it and take care of it" (Genesis 2:15). Before God cursed the ground because of sin, Adam must have considered his work refreshing and productive.

The Bible says we also "will serve" God in heaven (Revelation 22:3). Some will even "serve him day and night in his temple" (7:15). Like the Old Testament priests, we will be "a kingdom and priests to serve our God" (5:10).

In speaking of heaven, Wilbur Nelson said on his radio program, *The Morning Chapel Hour* (now called *Compassion Radio*), "I cannot tell you of all the glorious tasks which we may perform. But with talents greater than we now can imagine, we shall shine as the stars, sing as the angels, preach and praise and glorify and worship Him whose smile will be an eternal shining benediction, a glory far, far beyond words!"[4]

Think what it will be like to serve God without alarm clocks, heavy traffic, grumpy bosses, difficult coworkers, or physical exhaustion.

We Will Worship God

Although we will serve in various ways, we all will worship and praise our wonderful God and his Son Jesus Christ.

Author and pastor Don Baker believes such worship "will be spontaneous and genuine. It will encompass the whole universe. The *hallelujahs* and the *praise the Lords* and the *amens* will drown out all of the sounds of Heaven and earth. And we will all lose ourselves in the joy of telling our God how much we adore Him."[5]

Author and missionary leader J. Oswald Sanders agrees. He says, "The highest activity in heaven will be to ascribe to the triune God our spontaneous and unrestricted worship and adoration."[6]

In heaven we'll see so clearly what Jesus did by giving his life for us, we'll want to worship and praise him. When we see him face to face, we'll instinctively kneel in adoration. In fact, that's what heaven's inhabitants do. Scripture tells us that they "fall down before him" and "worship him who lives for ever and ever" (Revelation 4:10).

One of the most glorious pictures of heaven is of believers from every nation, tribe, people, and language probably shouting, "Salvation belongs to our God, who sits on the throne, and to the Lamb" (Revelation 7:10).

Angels will not only join in this worship but will demonstrate it for us. They fall on their faces and worship God, saying, "Amen! Praise and glory and wisdom and thanks and honor and power and strength be to our God for ever and ever. Amen!" (7:12).

Worship not only consists in speaking words of praise, but it also involves praising God by singing and playing instruments. During a Christmas concert one year, our church choir sang an especially beautiful anthem, accompanied by the orchestra. I watched a woman sitting in the audience, with tears streaming down her uplifted face. I wondered if music on this earth can stir hearts like this, what will the music of heaven be like?

The book of Revelation implies that music permeates

heaven. In his vision, the apostle John heard one group of believers singing "a new song of worship" (5:9–10). Then he heard "harpists playing their harps" (14:2) and another group singing "the song of God's servant Moses and of the Lamb" as they worshipped Christ (15:2–4). And of course he heard myriads of angels constantly singing praises to God.

Think what it will be like to listen to the heavenly choirs and orchestras, to play musical instruments beautifully, and to join the angels and other believers in singing glorious anthems of worship. Fortunately, no one will sing off-key or play discordant "rock band" music.

We Will Fellowship with Believers

In the early days of our mission in the Philippines, John and I worked with two other young couples at our southern center. Located in the country far from any town, we had no church and none of the usual activities associated with one.

So we rejoiced when time for the yearly conference came around. All the missionaries from across the islands gathered at this center. We delighted in seeing special friends again, in singing in a large group, and in hearing biblical messages from a guest speaker. Of course, we had business sessions, but the tedium was relieved afterwards by fast-moving volleyball games or swimming in our natural pool.

But in heaven we'll not only see believing friends and family members, but we'll also develop friendships and enjoy meals with believers from ages past. In fact, Jesus said that we will "feast with Abraham, Isaac and Jacob in the kingdom of heaven" (Matthew 8:11).

He also said we will "eat and drink" at his table in his kingdom (Luke 22:30).

Our most memorable meal will be the "wedding supper of the Lamb" when we believers, as Christ's bride, will feast with our Savior (Revelation 19:9).

Think what it will be to have dinner with Jesus, to talk with Moses and Joseph, to ask Paul questions, or to listen to beautiful Queen Esther's story.

We Will Learn More

To me, school was always a delight, as I enjoyed learning. When I was a freshman in high school, our English teacher, Miss Ruth Thompson, asked me to help her correct papers. I enjoyed working for this gracious, delightful lady and did so for eight years—all through high school and Bible college. From her, I learned the basics of punctuation, spelling, and the flow of the English language. Years later, I thanked her for setting me on the path of editing, proofreading, and writing—jobs I still enjoy.

Scripture suggests that we'll continue learning in heaven. The apostle Paul said, "Now I know in part; then I shall know fully, even as I am fully known" (1 Corinthians 13:12). He also prayed that believers would "grasp how wide and long and high and deep is the love of Christ, and to know this love that surpasses knowledge" (Ephesians 3:18–19). And that will happen fully only in heaven.

Think what it will be like to learn amazing new concepts and to use technology far greater than anything on earth. Perhaps we will explore heavenly libraries, read the best books from ages past, and take classes from angels. We will never forget names, never wonder where we put our keys, and never have "senior moments."

We Will Administer with Jesus

My present husband, Dan Weaver, was the ultimate administrator. Others in our mission recognized that he not only knew the principles of organization, but he also got along well with people. So he first became the director of the center on Mindanao, then the business manager in Manila, and then the director of the entire Philippine branch.

After a number of years, Dan directed the work in all of Asia. Still later, he took charge of the mission's large linguistic center in Dallas, Texas. Whatever he did, he always served like a pastor, caring for people and their needs.

In fact, God has not only been grooming Dan but all of us believers to be his administrators over the earth during and after the millennium.

Theologian and scholar Dallas Willard in *The Divine Conspiracy* says about reigning with Christ that "we should think of our destiny as being absorbed in a tremendously creative team effort, with unimaginably splendid leadership, on an inconceivably vast plane of activity, with ever more comprehensive cycles of production and enjoyment."[7]

According to our faithfulness now, God may put us in charge of certain cities or areas. Jesus explained this in his parable of the talents. The master gave his servants money to invest while he was gone. When he returned, he commended the first servant and said, "Well done, my good servant! . . . Because you have been trustworthy in a very small matter, take charge of ten cities" (Luke 19:17). He also commended the second servant.

Our reward for enduring trials and overcoming obstacles will be reigning with Christ: Paul assured us, "If we endure, we will also reign with him" (2 Timothy 2:12).

Furthermore, these administrative duties will continue forever: "His servants will serve him ... And they will reign for ever and ever" (Revelation 22:3, 5).

Amazingly, we'll administer without corrupt politicians, unworthy presidents, wrangling in a congress or senate, or an angry media.

We Will Rest from Our Labors

After cleaning and cooking most of a day, Nana would flop into an easy chair, stretch out her legs, and say, "Uff da! I'm tired." Soon she undid the laces and took off her shoes. Her corns were killing her. So I'm sure that in heaven she's enjoying a rest from her labors and has happy feet.

Up there, we'll know nothing of fatigue or exhaustion. In contrast to the ungodly who will have "no rest day or night" in hell (Revelation 14:11), those in heaven "will rest from their labor" (v. 13). Serving God there will seem like resting after the rigors of work on earth.

Just Think

We'll serve our wonderful Lord in every way possible. We'll join the angels in singing, worshipping, and praising the triune God. We'll fellowship and feast with other believers, we'll learn more, we'll administer with Jesus, and we'll rest from our earthly labors.

O That Will Be Glory

When all my labors and trials are o'er,
And I am safe on that beautiful shore,
Just to be near the dear Lord I adore,
Will through the ages be glory for me.

Oh, that will be glory for me,
Glory for me, glory for me,
When by His grace I shall look on His face,
That will be glory, be glory for me.

—Charles H. Gabriel (1856–1932)

CHAPTER 6
WILL WE BE REWARDED IN HEAVEN?

Faithful service brings rewards in this life as well as in the life to come.[1]

—J. Oswald Sanders

At the 2016 Summer Olympics in Rio de Janeiro, swimmer Michael Phelps won five gold medals, bringing his total count to twenty-three gold and twenty-eight medals overall. He was captain of the US team and carried the American flag in the Parade of Nations. As the most-decorated Olympian of all time, Phelps won the adulation of his country and the world.

In the Olympic games of ancient Greece, judges crowned winners with wreaths of laurel leaves. Of course, these crowns soon wilted.

In heaven, on the other hand, God will reward his faithful ones with golden crowns that will last forever. The Bible mentions five of these crowns: an enduring crown, a crown of glory, a crown of life, a crown of rejoicing, and a crown of righteousness.

An Enduring Crown

The Lord will award this enduring or "incorruptible" (KJV) crown for determination, self-discipline, and spiritual victory. Paul likened the Christian life to a race. He said, "Run in such a way as to get the prize. Everyone who competes in the games goes into strict training. They do it to get a crown that will not last; but we do it to get a crown that will last forever" (1 Corinthians 9:24-25).

After Dawson Trotman (1906-1956) became a Christian, he determined to witness to one person a day, memorize one verse a day, and spend one hour a day in prayer and reading the Bible.

In 1933 Trotman became acquainted with United States Navy sailor Lester Spencer and brought him to the Lord. Eventually, 135 sailors on Spencer's ship, the *USS West Virginia,* became Christians before the Japanese sank the ship at Pearl Harbor.

By the end of World War II, thousands of servicemen learned Trotman's basic principles of Christian discipleship.

Later, Trotman called his work The Navigators, a worldwide organization emphasizing personal follow-up of new converts, one-on-one training, and the multiplication of disciples. Its headquarters is in Glen Eyrie near Colorado Springs, Colorado. NavPress produces Bible-study books and study-aid materials.

After Trotman died while saving a young woman from drowning, *Time* magazine, in a July 2, 1956, article, "Always Holding Someone Up," called Trotman "the light and power of a movement that echoes the words of Scripture around the world."[2]

Dawson Trotman will surely receive an enduring crown for his determination, self-discipline, and victory.

A Crown of Glory

God has promised a crown of glory for Christian leadership and teaching. The apostle Peter urged pastors and teachers as the "shepherds of God's flock" to be "eager to serve" and to be "examples to the flock." Then he added, "And when the Chief Shepherd appears, you will receive the crown of glory that will never fade away" (1 Peter 5:2-4).

Reuben Archer (R. A.) Torrey (1856–1928), a highly educated scholar, preacher, teacher, evangelist, and author, was such a leader. He pastored several churches, taught in two Bible institutes, founded a conference center, held worldwide evangelistic campaigns, and wrote some forty books.

In 1886 evangelist Dwight L. Moody began what became known as the Moody Bible Institute in Chicago, a school for Christian workers. Three years later in 1889, he invited R. A. Torrey to become its superintendent. Torrey not only taught there for eleven years, but he also pastored the Chicago Avenue Church (now Moody Memorial Church) and added two thousand new members.

In 1908 he founded the Montrose Bible Conference in Montrose, Pennsylvania, in the Blue Ridge Mountains. That same year, the Bible Institute of Los Angeles (BIOLA) began. In 1912, Torrey became its dean and taught there for many years.

Amazingly, fifteen of Torrey's books on prayer, personal work, and Bible study have been republished and are still in print. His motto was, "Pray for great things, expect great things, work for great things, but above all pray."[3]

R. A. Torrey will surely receive a crown of glory for his faithful leadership, teaching, and writing.

A Crown of Life

God will give the crown of life to those who love him and remain true to him through trials, persecution, even martyrdom. James, Jesus's brother, wrote to the Jewish believers who had been scattered by Herod Agrippa's persecution (ca. AD 44): "Blessed is the one who perseveres under trial because, having stood the test, that person will receive the crown of life that the Lord has promised to those who love him" (James 1:12).

The general population of Smyrna in Asia Minor (now Izmir, Turkey) worshipped the Roman emperor as a god, so Jesus, through the apostle John, warned believers of a coming persecution. He told them to "be faithful, even to the point of death, and I will give you the crown of life" (Revelation 2:10 NIV 1984).

According to *The Martyrdom of Polycarp,* the eighty-six-year-old bishop of Smyrna, *Polycarp,* received the heavenly crown of life some fifty years after John died. His enemies tied Bishop Polycarp to a stake and then set it on fire for not worshipping Caesar. When the flames failed to touch him, he was then stabbed to death.[4] He, along with persecuted modern-day Christians, will receive crowns of life.

A Crown of Rejoicing

God will give crowns of rejoicing to those who share the gospel with others. Paul said that those he had led to Christ were his "hope, or joy, or crown of rejoicing" (1 Thessalonians 2:19 KJV).

Young farm boy and vice president of Youth for Christ, Billy Graham (1918–2018), began his first evangelistic crusade on September 25, 1949, in a large tent in downtown Los Angeles. He, along with friends Cliff Barrows and

George Beverly Shea, planned to hold the meetings for only three weeks. But things changed when the Hearst newspapers gave front-page accounts of the meetings and the conversion of several famous personalities.

So the crusade was held over to eight weeks, with three thousand people accepting Christ. Crowds of up to fifteen thousand crowded the tent, with another six thousand standing outside.

Thirty-year-old Billy gave God all the glory. The prayers of many had launched a worldwide ministry that would shake the world.

Billy and his team went on to hold crusades in almost every nation. In 1957 during his sixteen-week series in New York City, 2,357,400 people attended, and 61,148 made decisions for Christ. In Hong Kong, Graham's November 1990 messages in person and by satellite reached one hundred million people in thirty Asian countries with countless numbers receiving Christ as Savior.[5]

Billy's son Franklin now holds crusades and leads Samaritan's Purse. The Graham team continues to reach the world by radio and TV programs, books, a magazine, and motion pictures.

About his success as an evangelist, Graham said, "If God should take his hands off my life, my lips would turn to clay." He added, "I feel so undeserving of all the Spirit has done, because the work has been God's, not man's. I want no credit or glory. I want the Lord Jesus to have it all."[6]

No doubt, Billy Graham will receive a crown of rejoicing for winning others to the Lord.

A Crown of Righteousness

God will give crowns of righteousness to those who

finish their God-given work and look forward to Christ's return. Paul was one of these. Using boxing and running in the ancient Greek games as metaphors, he said, "I have fought the good fight, I have finished the race, I have kept the faith. Now there is in store for me the crown of righteousness, which the Lord, the righteous Judge, will award to me on that day—and not only to me, but also to all who have longed for his appearing" (2 Timothy 4:7-8).

In 1901 missionary and author Amy Carmichael (1867–1951) founded the Dohnavur Fellowship in India. She and her fellow workers rescued children, who had been dedicated by their families to temple prostitution, and raised them in a godly environment.

After thirty-seven years of active service, she fell and broke a leg so seriously that she scarcely left her room for the next twenty years. She had written several books before, but from then on, she wrote many more, and God used them to bless and challenge others around the world.[7]

One of her many poems closes with these words: "Of all our prayers this is the sum: O come, Lord Jesus, come."[8]

Amy Carmichael will undoubtedly receive a crown of righteousness for finishing her God-given work as she looked forward to Christ's return.

Just Think

Some of us will receive enduring crowns, crowns of glory, crowns of life, crowns of rejoicing, or crowns of righteousness.

If we are so fortunate as to receive crowns, what should our responses be? In gratitude and praise, we will fall at Jesus's feet in worship and give them back to him. Like the twenty-four elders in Revelation, we will lay our "crowns before the throne and say, 'You are worthy, our Lord and God, to receive glory and honor and power, for you created all things, and by your will they were created and have their being'" (Revelation 4:10-11).

Still Will We Trust

Still will be trust, though earth seem dark and dreary,
And the heart faint beneath His chastening rod;
Though rough and steep our pathway, worn and weary,
Still will we trust in God!

Let us press on, in patient self-denial,
Accept the hardship, shrink not from the loss:
Our portion lies beyond the hour of trial,
Our crown beyond the cross.

—W. H. Burleigh (1812–1871)

Chapter 7

WILL WE KNOW EACH OTHER IN HEAVEN?

Several references in the Bible indicate that we shall know each other in Heaven.[1]
—James T. Jeremiah

As I have told about previously, Mother put my brother, John, and me in dormitories at a boarding school and left us to fend for ourselves while she went overseas to do missionary work. She was gone for ten years and never came back during that time.

When we were in college, Mother wrote us, saying that she was returning. She would arrive by a passenger ship in Vancouver, BC, on a certain date and hoped we could meet her.

Ten years is a long time to be apart, and we had our wonderments. John was a skinny kid when Mother left, and now he was a young man. I had been wearing Sloppy Joe sweaters and saddle shoes then and was now a young lady. Would she recognize us? Would we recognize her?

Our stomachs churned as we stood on the dock and watched people hurrying down the gangplank then rushing to greet family and friends.

Finally, we saw an older woman pick her way slowly down. *Was that really Mother?* I wondered. She had always been active, but now she was showing her age. A younger woman helped her and carried some of her things.

John and I hung back, not quite sure how to act with this woman. But when we saw her looking around, we walked to her. "Hi, Mother," I said as I gave her a slight hug.

She set down her bundles and recognized me, but she studied the tall young man beside me with a baffled look.

"Mother, this is Jock," I said. I felt as if I were introducing her to someone she didn't know.

"Oh, my goodness!" she said to him. "You've grown up! I didn't recognize you." Then she gave him a real hug.

Although we were glad to see Mother, John and I both felt as if we didn't really know her. She had been gone during our growing-up years and hadn't been part of our lives.

But we won't have such feelings in heaven. Our arrival there will be a time of rejoicing when we see God the Father and our Lord Jesus Christ first of all. Then we will greet family, friends, and others. The question is, will we really recognize and know them? Scripture seems to indicate that we will. Here are some specifics:

We'll Know More in Heaven

The apostle Paul said, "For now we see only a reflection as in a mirror; then we shall see face to face. Now I know in part; then I shall know fully, even as I am fully known" (1 Corinthians 13:12). So we'll know more in heaven than we know here.

Old Testament Saints

Jesus declared that Old Testament saints are alive and well in heaven. He said, "Have you not read what God said to you, 'I am the God of Abraham, the God of Isaac, and the God of Jacob?' He is not the God of the dead but of the living" (Matthew 22:31–32).

Apparently, we believers will get to know such notables. Jesus said that we will feast with Abraham, Isaac and Jacob in the kingdom of heaven" (Matthew 8:11).

David and His Son

When King David and Bathsheba's baby boy became ill, David wept, fasted, and prayed for six days. On the seventh day, the child died, and the king washed, changed his clothes, and ate.

The servants asked why he did this, and he replied, "I will go to him, but he will not return to me" (2 Samuel 12:23).

David fully expected to know his son in heaven.

Saul and Samuel

Before what turned out to be King Saul's last battle with the Philistines, he became desperate for guidance. God wouldn't answer him because of his sins, so Saul asked the medium at Endor to bring the prophet Samuel from the dead so he could ask him what to do.

When an old man appeared, "Saul knew it was Samuel, and he bowed down and prostrated himself with his face to the ground" (1 Samuel 28:14).

The Disciples on the Mount of Transfiguration

One day when Jesus took Peter, James, and John up a high mountain, he was transfigured before them. "His face shone like the sun, and his clothes became as white as the light. Just then there appeared before them Moses and Elijah, talking with Jesus" (Matthew 17:2–3).

Apparently the disciples recognized these Old Testament saints, for Peter in his confusion, said, "Lord, it is good for us to be here. If you wish, I will put up three shelters—one for you, one for Moses and one for Elijah" (v. 4).

The Rich Man and Lazarus

Jesus told about a beggar named Lazarus who begged for food from a rich man's doorstep. When the beggar died, angels carried him to paradise to join Abraham.

The rich man also died and went to Hades where fire tormented him. He pled with Abraham to send Lazarus to cool his tongue with a little water. But Abraham said that was impossible (*see* Luke 16:23–24).

Interestingly enough, the rich man, Lazarus, and Abraham all recognized each other.

The Dying Thief

When Jesus was crucified between two thieves on the cross, one of them shouted, "Aren't you the Messiah? Save yourself and us!" (Luke 23:39).

The other criminal reminded him that they were being punished justly, then he put his faith in Christ, for he added, "Jesus, remember me when you come into your kingdom" (v. 42).

Jesus responded, "Truly I tell you, today you will be with me in paradise" (v. 43).

Inherent in his promise was the understanding that he and the thief would know each other in heaven.

Stephen Before His Death

When Stephen preached to the Jewish leaders, they grew so furious that they stoned him. As he lay dying, he looked up to heaven and saw Jesus standing to welcome him (*see* Acts 7:56). Stephen obviously recognized his Lord.

People Recognized Jesus After His Resurrection

After Jesus rose from the dead, he appeared to various

believers in his heavenly body, and they eventually recognized him. In heaven we'll have bodies similar to his resurrected body.

The fact that people recognized him in his new body here assures us that we'll not only recognize him in heaven, but we'll recognize each other too.

Mary Magdalene

After Jesus's resurrection, he was standing near the tomb. Through her tears, Mary Magdalene didn't recognize him and thought he was the gardener (*see* John 20:13).

But when he called her name, she recognized his voice and cried out, "Teacher!" (v. 16).

The Two Believers on the Road to Emmaus

Two believers talked about Jesus's death as they walked to the village of Emmaus.

When Jesus joined them and pointed out what Scripture said concerning himself, they didn't recognize him. But when he joined them for a light meal, they realized who he was before he suddenly disappeared (*see* Luke 24:15–31).

The Disciples

On the first evening after Jesus's resurrection, the disciples met together behind locked doors for fear of the Jewish leaders.

When Jesus suddenly walked through the door, they were terrified. He showed them his hands and side to prove who he was.

Thomas was not with them, however, and refused to believe that the others had seen him. So a week later, Jesus again appeared and let Thomas put his fingers on his hands and side. Thomas's doubts disappeared when he recognized his Lord (*see* John 20:19–28).

Later one night when several disciples fished, they

caught nothing. Early the next morning, they saw a man standing on the shore but didn't realize that he was Jesus.

At his instruction to throw their net on the right side of the boat, they caught so many fish that they couldn't pull them in.

John recognized him first, but they all did when Jesus invited them for breakfast (*see* John 21:4–22).

Jesus continued to appear to his disciples "and gave many convincing proofs that he was alive. He appeared to them over a period of forty days" (Acts 1:3).

Five Hundred Other People

The apostle Paul tells us that Jesus also "appeared to more than five hundred of the brothers and sisters at the same time" (1 Corinthians 15:6). He explained that at the time, most of them were still living and could attest to this appearance.

Pastor and author David Jeremiah says, "We will be recognizable in heaven, just as Christ was recognizable to His disciples when He returned to earth after His resurrection (John 21:12–13)."[2]

Present-Day Recognitions

Occasionally, present-day people see believers who have died. For instance, when our friend Doris Fell cared for her dying mother, the elderly lady looked across the room one day and said, "There's Julie!" She recognized her believing granddaughter, who had passed away a few years earlier. Julie was dressed all in white, with her usual long flowing hair.

Shortly afterward, the dying woman said to Doris, "And there's Mother standing in the corner!" She added regretfully, "You can't see her, can you?"

One day I was caring for my beloved Nana during her final illness. She looked up to the ceiling and said, "There's Donald, and he's in his Coast Guard uniform!" Perhaps her nephew, who had died of a brain tumor a few years previously, was dressed in white because he had been a believer, and that caused Nana to think he was wearing his uniform.

In chapter one, I told about missionary-linguist Len Newell seeing family and friends gathered at one of heaven's gates to welcome him as he was dying. No doubt some were former Ifugao headhunters he had won to the Lord. He obviously recognized everyone he saw because he called out their names before he slipped away.

Missionary leader J. Oswald Sanders in his book *Heaven: Better by Far*, says, "One of the anticipatory joys of heaven is the prospect of reunion . . . .Family relationships among believers will not be broken. Death will not destroy our connection with the past."[3]

Just Think

Not only will God the Father and our Lord Jesus welcome us when we arrive in heaven, but our believing loved ones and other saints will welcome us too. And we'll know them all!

When the Mists Have Rolled Away
When the mists have rolled in splendor
From the beauty of the hills,
And the sunlight falls in gladness
On the rivers and the rills,
We recall our Father's promise
In the rainbow of the spray:

We shall know each other better
When the mists have rolled away.

We shall know, as we are known,
Never more to walk alone,
In the dawning of the morning
Of that bright and happy day,
We shall know each other better
When the mists have rolled away.

We shall come with joy and gladness,
We shall gather round the throne,
Face to face with those that love us,
We shall know as we are known.
And the song of our redemption
Shall resound through endless day
When the shadows have departed
And the mists have rolled away.
—Annie Herbert Barker (1844–1932)

CHAPTER 8

CAN PEOPLE IN HEAVEN OBSERVE US?

Each day, each moment, a million eyes are watching us.[1]
—Randy Alcorn

On January 24, 1949, Senate Chaplain and pastor of the New York Avenue Church in Washington, DC, Peter Marshall was rushed to the hospital with chest pains. During the night, he passed away.

Early the next morning, a doctor called Peter's wife, Catherine, to tell her that her husband had just died of a heart attack.

"Don't move him!" she replied. "Don't touch him until I get there."

When she arrived, a young doctor showed her to Peter's room and asked, "Are you *sure* you want to go in there alone?"

"Oh, yes," she said.

When Catherine entered the room, she was instantly aware that she was not alone. Though she couldn't understand how, she knew Peter was observing her. Beside him was "another Presence of transcendent glory—the Lord he had served through long years."[2]

Yet the glory of that realization was not to last. At a precise moment, the two presences withdrew. She felt that the spirits of Jesus and her husband Peter had waited to comfort and reassure her.[3]

Can people in heaven observe us on earth? Scripture has a few instances of this. Consider, for example, the following:

Samuel Observed Saul

As we saw in the previous chapter, the prophet Samuel knew what was happening on earth. When he was briefly brought back, he was aware of what King Saul had done and what he had failed to do.

When the prophet demanded to know why the king had disturbed him, Saul complained about the distress he was in. "The Philistines are fighting against me, and God has departed from me. He no longer answers me, either by prophets or by dreams. So I have called on you to tell me what to do" (1 Samuel 28:15).

Samuel replied, "Because you did not obey the Lord or carry out his fierce wrath against the Amalekites, the Lord has done this to you today" (v. 18).

Moses and Elijah Observed Jesus

When Moses and Elijah met Jesus on the Mount of Transfiguration, they also knew what was happening on earth. They talked with Jesus "about his departure, which he was about to bring to fulfillment at Jerusalem" (Luke 9:31).

Yet Moses had been dead for more than 1,400 years, and Elijah had been whirled up to heaven over six centuries before Jesus was born.

Believers in Heaven Observe Conversions

Jesus told his followers a parable about a shepherd who had a hundred sheep, and one of them had wandered away. The shepherd left the ninety-nine and searched for the missing member of his flock. Once home, he called his friends and family together and said, "Rejoice with me; I have found my lost sheep" (Luke 15:6).

Jesus then applied the story to the heavenly realm where both angels and believers praise God whenever a person on earth turns to him. Jesus said, "I tell you that in the same way there will be more rejoicing in heaven over one sinner who repents than over ninety-nine righteous persons who do not need to repent" (v. 7).

Several years ago, I was taking care of my older sister, Jean, who was dying of cancer. I hadn't been around her for many years, since she previously lived in a distant city, but I knew that my late mother and Nana were concerned about her spiritual condition.

After choir practice at church one evening, I talked with one of the members, an oncologist, about her. "She hasn't eaten for a week," I said. "How long can she last?"

He shook his head. "Probably a few days, but she can go anytime."

So when I got home, I felt a strong urge to talk with her. "Jeannie," I said, "I know that you'll want to go to heaven when you die and see Mother, Nana, and Dad."

She nodded her head.

So I held her hand and led her in the sinner's prayer, speaking slowly and clearly.

Even though she couldn't respond audibly, I was sure that she really did come to the Lord. His presence permeated the room.

As I went for a walk afterwards, I had a strong sense of Mother and Nana leaning over the walls of heaven, saying, "Good for you!"

Preacher Charles Spurgeon wrote, "The birthday of every Christian is a sonnet day in heaven . . . There are days—good days in heaven, days of sonnet, red-letter days of overflowing adoration. And these are days when the shepherd brings home the lost sheep upon his shoulder, when the church has swept her house and found the lost piece of money, for then are these friends and neighbors called together, and they rejoice with joy unspeakable and full of glory over one sinner that repenteth."[4]

Believers in Heaven Observe Judgments

Apparently, believers in heaven are aware of certain events on earth. For instance, when God destroys Babylon, an angel says, "Rejoice over her, you heavens! Rejoice, you people of God! Rejoice, apostles and prophets! For God has judged her with the judgment she imposed on you" (Revelation 18:20).

Moreover, a "great multitude in heaven" shouts, "Hallelujah! Salvation and glory and power belong to our God, for true and just are his judgments" (19:1–2).

Believers in Heaven Are Like Spectators

The writer of the book of Hebrews pictures a huge sports stadium filled with spectators in heaven watching believers on earth as in a foot race. He says, "Therefore, since we are surrounded by such a great cloud of witnesses... let us run with perseverance the race marked out for us" (Hebrews 12:1).

One commentary says: "The image is from a 'race,'

an image common even in Palestine from the time of the Graeco-Macedonian empire, which introduced such Greek usages as national games. The 'witnesses' answer to the spectators pressing round to see the competitors in their contest for the prize." Such witnesses "ought to increase our earnestness, testifying, as they do, to God's faithfulness."[5]

Author Randy Alcorn suggests, "These witnesses are the saints who've gone before us. The imagery suggests that those saints, the spiritual 'athletes' of old, are now watching us and cheering us on from the stands of heaven. They're said not merely to have preceded us but to 'surround' us. Each day, each moment, a million eyes are watching us."[6]

Sometimes we may be aware of the presence of believers who have gone to heaven. My firefighter son, Ken, told me about an experience he and a friend had when they fought forest fires in Eastern Washington. Flames moving swiftly down a ridge began to encircle them in a ring of fire.

The men panicked. They had heard about other firefighters who had died not far away.

As he told me this, Ken's eyes filled with tears. "Mom," he said, "suddenly I felt Dad's presence. He was right beside me, comforting, reassuring me. And then I saw a narrow way of escape. We ran out of there alive!"

Just Think

As we run our Christian race, our family members, friends, and other believers in heaven are cheering us on!

When We All Get to Heaven
Sing the wondrous love of Jesus,
Sing His mercy and His grace;
In the mansions bright and blessed

He'll prepare for us a place.

When we all get to heaven,
What a day of rejoicing that will be!
When we all see Jesus,
We'll sing and shout the victory!

Onward to the prize before us!
Soon His beauty we'll behold;
Soon the pearly gates will open;
We shall tread the streets of gold.
—Eliza E. Hewitt (1851–1920)

CHAPTER 9

WHO ARE ANGELS, AND WHAT DO THEY DO IN HEAVEN?

The angels walk the floor of heaven tonight,
Their garments trailing splendor as they pass.[1]
—Grace Noll Crowell

In January 1956, five young American missionaries—Nate Saint, Jim Elliot, Ed McCully, Pete Fleming, and Roger Youderian—penetrated Ecuador's dark jungles to bring the gospel to the Auca (now called the Huaorani) tribe. In spite of the missionaries's overtures of friendship, the natives brutally speared them and threw their bodies in the river.

Forty years later when Steve Saint, Nate's son, visited these people, he learned what happened after that attack. The warriors who had participated in the deaths told him they had been frightened when they saw shining figures in the trees and heard them singing. After becoming Christians, the natives identified the bright figures as angels and the music like the choral singing they later heard on phonograph records.[2]

Although this took place on earth, it gives us a glimpse of angels as "bright figures" singing together beautifully like they do in heaven.

The Bible fairly whispers with the swish of angelic wings, but we have questions: Who are they? What do they look like? How many are there? How are they organized? Do they have names? What do they do in heaven?

To answer these questions, let's see what the Bible says about them.

Who Are Angels?

The Hebrew word for *angel* in the Old Testament is *mal'akh*, and the Greek word in the New Testament is *aggelos*. Both words mean "messenger." The writer of Hebrews calls them "ministering spirits" (Hebrews 1:14).

The Bible refers to angels directly or indirectly nearly three hundred times. In his book *Angels: God's Secret Agents*, Billy Graham says that angels "are God's messengers whose chief business is to carry out His orders in the world . . . He has designated and empowered them as holy deputies to perform works of righteousness."[3]

God created these heavenly beings. The apostle Paul said, "For by him all things were created: things in heaven and on earth, visible and invisible, whether thrones or powers or rulers or authorities; all things were created through him and for him" (Colossians 1:16).

We know that angels were on the scene when God created the earth and humankind. He said to the prophet Job, "Where were you when I laid the earth's foundation . . . while the morning stars sang together and all the angels shouted for joy?" (Job 38:4, 7).

What Do Angels Look Like?

Angels are neither male nor female. Jesus clearly pointed this out when he said, "At the resurrection people will neither marry nor be given in marriage; they will be like the angels in heaven" (Matthew 22:30).

Nowhere in the Bible are angels described as winged women or chubby cherubs, as often depicted by artists. Instead, they appear in a variety of forms, sometimes as awe-inspiring masculine-looking beings, who create fear, and other times like ordinary people.

The prophet Daniel gave a detailed description of an awesome angel in a vision: "I looked up and there before me was a man dressed in linen, with a belt of fine gold from Uphaz around his waist. His body was like topaz, his face like lightning, his eyes like flaming torches, his arms and legs like the gleam of burnished bronze, and his voice like the sound of a multitude" (Daniel 10:5–6). The prophet said, "I had no strength left, my face turned deathly pale and I was helpless" (v. 8). Then the angel said, "Do not be afraid, Daniel" (v. 12).

After Jesus's resurrection, "an angel of the Lord came down from heaven and, going to the tomb, rolled back the stone and sat on it. His appearance was like lightning, and his clothes were white as snow. The guards were so afraid of him that they shook and became like dead men" (Matthew 28:2–4).

In a vision, the apostle John "saw another mighty angel coming down from heaven. He was robed in a cloud, with a rainbow above his head; his face was like the sun, and his legs were like fiery pillars" (Revelation 10:1).

On the other hand, angels can take on the appearance of ordinary human beings. Two angels looking like men appeared to Abraham (*see* Genesis 18:2) and later arrived at Lot's home in Sodom (*see* 19:1).

Looking like a man, an angel came to Manoah and his wife to announce Samson's birth. Only when the angel ascended in a flame of fire did they realize who he was (*see* Judges 13:11, 20).

On another occasion, an angel sat under an oak tree seemingly like an ordinary man before he commissioned Gideon for battle (*see* Judges 6:11).

In some present-day instances that I will tell about in the next chapter, angels have looked like Asian men, women flight attendants, a well-dressed Russian man, an indigenous Ecuadorian woman, a Filipina nun, a Chinese man, a Norwegian Bible distributor, armored warriors, and a nurse.

How Many Angels Are There?

No one can ever begin to count the number of angels. Scripture refers to "thousands upon thousands of angels in joyful assembly" in the heavenly Jerusalem (Hebrews 12:22).

John wrote, "Then I looked and heard the voice of many angels, numbering thousands upon thousands, and ten thousand times ten thousand" (Revelation 5:11).

In his book *Answers to Questions About Heaven*, pastor and author David Jeremiah tells us that ten thousand was the highest numerical figure used in the Greek language. He suggests, "'Ten thousand times ten thousand' may have been John's way of describing an inexpressibly large company of angels."[4]

When Jesus was arrested, he said to his disciples, "Do you think I cannot call on my Father, and he will at once put at my disposal more than twelve legions of angels?" (Matthew 26:53). Since a Roman legion had 6,000 soldiers, Jesus was speaking of 72,000 angels who could come to his aid at a moment's notice.

How Are Angels Organized?

Cherubim

Angels who are called *cherubim* surround God's throne and guard his holiness. In his book *What the Bible Says About Angels*, David Jeremiah suggests, "Perhaps cherubim (the Hebrew plural of cherub) are the real workhorses among the angels as they fulfill their role as royal guards in service to the King."[5]

When God banned Adam and Eve from the garden of Eden after they sinned, he placed "cherubim and a flaming sword flashing back and forth to guard the way to the tree of life" (Genesis 3:24).

God also told Moses to "make two cherubim out of hammered gold" to put on the ark of the covenant in the tabernacle. "The cherubim are to have their wings spread upward, overshadowing the cover with them" (Exodus 25:18, 20). Figures of cherubim were richly embroidered on the tabernacle curtains (*see* 26:31). Statues of golden cherubim later were part of Solomon's temple.

Seraphim or Seraphs

Angels called *seraphim* or *seraphs* ("burning ones") hover around God's throne. They sing his praises and wait to do his bidding. The Bible mentions them only once.

After a vision of God's glory, the prophet Isaiah said, "I saw the Lord, high and exalted, seated on a throne; and the train of his robe filled the temple. Above him were seraphim, each with six wings: With two wings they covered their faces, with two they covered their feet, and with two they were flying" (Isaiah 6:1–2).

The seraphim called to one another and said, "Holy, holy, holy is the Lord Almighty; the whole earth is full of his glory" (v. 3).

The presence of God's glorious holiness overcame the prophet Isaiah with a realization of his sinfulness. But one of the seraphim flew to him with a burning coal, touching his mouth and saying, "Your guilt is taken away and your sin atoned for" (v. 7).

Other Angelic Ranks

The Bible mentions other positions that angels hold. Paul spoke about God seating Christ "far above all rule and authority, power and dominion, and every name that is invoked, not only in the present age but also in the one to come" (Ephesians 1:20–21).

Peter says that Christ is seated "at God's right hand— with angels, authorities and powers in submission to him" (1 Peter 3:22).

Do Angels Have Names?

The Bible mentions only three angels by name— Michael, Gabriel, and Lucifer.

Michael

Michael is the only archangel, for he is called "*the* archangel" in verse 9 of Jude (*emphasis added*). The prefix *arch* suggests that he is the chief, the highest in rank of all angels. His name means, "Who is like God?"

David Jeremiah calls Michael "the royal champion of God's people."[6] A mighty warrior, he fights God's battles against evil powers in the spirit world.

In Daniel's day, Michael fought against demons that

controlled Persia (now Iran) and Greece (Daniel 10:13, 21). In speaking to Daniel, another angel calls Michael "one of the chief princes" (v. 13) and then "your prince," referring to his guardianship of Israel (v. 21).

John wrote of a "war in heaven" where "Michael and his angels fought against the dragon [Satan], and the dragon and his fallen angels fought back" (Revelation 12:7 TLB).

Furthermore, Michael will announce Jesus's second coming to take believers, dead or alive, to himself: "For the Lord himself will come down from heaven, with a loud command, with the voice of the archangel and with the trumpet call of God, and the dead in Christ will rise first. After that, we who are still alive and are left will be caught up together with them in the clouds to meet the Lord in the air. And so will we be with the Lord forever" (1 Thessalonians 4:16–17).

Gabriel

The angel Gabriel ("mighty one of God") is God's messenger and stands in the presence of the Almighty. As the announcing angel, he has conveyed and interpreted the Lord's messages to people.

For instance, after God gave Daniel visions of the future, Gabriel appeared and said, "I have now come to give you insight and understanding" (Daniel 9:22).

Gabriel also appeared to the priest Zechariah in the temple. The priest was frightened when he saw the angel, but Gabriel said, "Do not be afraid, Zechariah; your prayer has been heard. Your wife Elizabeth will bear you a son, and you are to call him John" (Luke 1:13).

When Zechariah couldn't believe this, the angel explained who he was and why he had come: "I am Gabriel. I stand in the presence of God, and I have been sent to speak to you and to tell you this good news" (v. 19). The son was later called John the Baptist.

But the most wonderful announcement Gabriel ever made was when God sent him to a young woman named Mary. She was startled, but he said, "Do not be afraid, Mary; you have found favor with God. You will conceive and give birth to a son, and you are to call him Jesus. He will be great and will be called the Son of the Most High. The Lord God will give him the throne of his father David, and he will reign over Jacob's descendants forever; and his kingdom will never end" (Luke 1:30–32).

Soon after, when her relative, Elizabeth, gave her a beautiful prophetic greeting, Mary responded in kind:

Mary's Magnificat
Luke 1:46–53

My soul glorifies the Lord;
My spirit rejoices in my King.
He remembers my low estate.
His praises do I sing!

The Mighty One has done great things,
And holy is his name.
His mercy reaches all mankind.
His love is ever the same.

He does great and mighty deeds.
He brings down rulers and kings.
He raises up the humble
And fills the hungry with good things.
　　　　　　　—Agnes C. Lawless

Lucifer

God created all angels as good, but Lucifer, a leading prince in heaven, wanted to be like God himself. Full of pride, he declared, "I will ascend above the tops of the clouds; I will make myself like the Most High" (Isaiah 14:14). He then incited a third of the angels into his scheme of rebellion (*see* Revelation 12:4).

Of course, the Lord could not tolerate sin in heaven, so he expelled them. They became fallen angels and are Satan's agents on earth. Paul warned us that Satan himself "masquerades as an angel of light" (2 Corinthians 11:14).

Moreover, God imprisoned certain angels in a section of hell, where he will later judge them (*see* 2 Peter 2:4).

What Do Angels Do in Heaven?

Angels Praise and Worship God

In his vision, John saw thousands of angels encircling God's throne and singing, "Worthy is the Lamb, who was slain, to receive power and wealth and wisdom and strength and honor and glory and praise!" (Revelation 5:12).

Angels Serve God

The psalmist David gives a vivid picture of God's agents in the universe. "Praise the Lord, you his angels, you mighty ones who do his bidding, who obey his word. Praise the Lord, all his heavenly hosts, you his servants who do his will" (Psalm 103:20–22).

Angels Fight God's Battles

Angels fight God's battles against evil powers in the spirit world. For more about this, refer to the previous section about the archangel Michael, who leads the heavenly hosts against Satan and his forces (*see* Daniel 10:12–13 and Revelation 12:7).

When King Sennacherib of Assyria tried to overthrow Jerusalem, godly King Hezekiah prayed earnestly. The result? "That night the angel of the Lord went out and put to death a hundred and eighty-five thousand in the Assyrian camp" (2 Kings 19:35).

Angels Rejoice at the Salvation of Unbelievers

Jesus said, "There is rejoicing in the presence of the angels of God over one sinner who repents" (Luke 15:10).

Just Think

Angels are God's secret servants. They have varied forms, and there are thousands upon thousands of them. They are well organized, but we know of only three names. In heaven, angels praise and worship God, serve him, fight his battles, and rejoice at the conversion of unbelievers.

Won't it be wonderful to see angels in action when we get to our heavenly home?

Angel Voices, Ever Singing

Angel voices, ever singing
Round Thy throne of light;
Angel harps, forever ringing,
Rest not day nor night.
Thousands only live to bless Thee
And confess Thee, Lord of might.

Honor, glory, might, and merit,
Thine shall ever be,
Father, Son, and Holy Spirit,
Blessed Trinity!
Of the best that Thou hast given
Earth and heaven render Thee.

—Francis Pott (1832–1909)

CHAPTER 10
WHAT DO ANGELS DO ON EARTH?

Through what angels say and do, God personally expresses His friendship to us and His fatherhood and much more.[1]
—David Jeremiah

My friend, Lydia Harris, told me about her father's angel experience. Pastor Nicolai Siemens wanted to leave Communist Russia with his family in 1929. But while he waited in Moscow for passports, authorities imprisoned him because he was a minister. Later, they miraculously released him, even though they had sent other prisoners to Siberia.

Now almost penniless, Nicolai was traveling by train to visit relatives. Deeply disturbed as he rode, he prayed, "Oh, God, please help us! We're totally destitute. How can we ever escape this country?"

Suddenly, a striking, well-dressed man sat down beside Nicolai, surprisingly because the passenger car was nearly empty. Before long, the stranger handed him a large sum of money then walked down the aisle and disappeared.

Nearly overcome, Nicolai clutched the money to his chest and prayed, "Oh, thank you, God! Thank you!" He felt certain that this mysterious stranger was not only an angel but that God would continue to meet their needs.

When Nicolai, his wife, and their son Abe received their passports, they passed safely under Moscow's Red Gate into Latvia on December 3, 1929. Two years later, they traveled by ship to freedom in America—largely because God had sent the angel on the train.

In this chapter, we will see how God often uses angels to minister to believers. They can provide, convey his messages, guide and help, encourage, protect, and finally escort believers to heaven when they die.

Angels Provide for Believers

The Bible tells about God's provision for the prophet Elijah through an angel. When wicked Queen Jezebel threatened to kill him, he ran for his life into the desert. He lay down under a bush and fell asleep. "All at once, an angel touched him and said, 'Get up and eat.' He looked around, and there by his head was some bread baked over hot coals, and a jar of water. He ate and drank and then lay down again" (1 Kings 19:5–6).

The angel returned and gave Elijah another meal before God sent the prophet on a long trip.

Angels Convey God's Messages

In the previous chapter, we told about Gabriel's announcements to Zechariah and to the Virgin Mary. But an angel also spoke several times in dreams to Mary's husband, Joseph.

The first occasion was before Joseph and Mary were officially married, and an angel told Joseph to take pregnant Mary as his wife (Matthew 1:20–21).

When King Herod wanted to kill the young Jesus, the angel directed Joseph to take him and his mother to Egypt (2:13).

Then after Herod was dead, the angel told Joseph to return with his little family to Israel (2:20). But when Joseph heard that Herod's wicked son was the ruler in Judea, he was afraid to go to that region. After being warned in a dream (no doubt by a heavenly messenger), Joseph withdrew to Galilee instead and settled in the town of Nazareth (2:22–23).

One of the more remarkable angelic announcements was made to shepherds in the fields outside Bethlehem after Jesus was born. "The angel said to them, 'Do not be afraid. I bring you good news that will cause great joy for all the people. Today in the town of David a Savior has been born to you; he is the Messiah, the Lord'" (Luke 2:10–11).

Angels Guide and Help Believers

"Are not all angels ministering spirits sent to serve those who will inherit salvation?" (Hebrews 1:14).

Several years ago, our friend, Jody Lynn, was scheduled to fly to Japan with business colleagues from the Boeing Company. But she missed her flight. Instead, she flew on a shuttle to Vancouver, BC, to meet her plane before it left for Japan.

When Jody deplaned in Vancouver, a woman dressed in a white blouse and dark-blue skirt waited while the plane unloaded. Jody asked her for help, and the attendant quickly found the luggage and got it transferred to the international flight. Then she walked Jody to the plane, boarded with her, and showed her to a seat.

Jody turned around to thank her, but the woman had

disappeared. Jody felt sure that God had provided an angel to help her on her way.

In another instance, my late husband, Dick Elkins, had to fly from the Philippines to California for mission board meetings. Before he left Manila, he told friends that his back was hurting and asked them to pray that he would be able to lift his heavy luggage without harm when he landed.

One lady told him, "I believe God is going to send an angel to help you."

When Dick arrived in Los Angeles, he waited for his luggage at the baggage-claim area. Soon the two bags spun towards him, and he reached out to grab them.

Just then a young Asian man touched his arm and said, "No, sir, let me get them for you." He lifted both heavy bags, carried them to the street, and shoved them into a waiting taxi.

Dick thanked him and reached for his billfold to tip him, but the man had disappeared. God had indeed sent an angel to help him.

In his book, *Time and Again*, Dick told about a Manobo man who died far from home, and his body was taken to the city morgue. His sisters and mother arrived to take care of his remains.

The morgue manager was gruff. "Where is your casket and truck?" he demanded.

"We have no casket, no truck, and no money," a sister replied.

"But you can't just leave his body here!" he said. "If you don't take it away by 3:00 o'clock tomorrow afternoon, you'll all go to jail."

"God will provide for us," she answered. She and the

other women spent the night praying outside the morgue, in spite of the manager's verbal abuse.

Just before the deadline, a little nun drove up in a truck and told the women why she was there: "Last night I couldn't sleep. Suddenly, an angel appeared to me and said, 'Get a truck and a coffin, and go to the morgue.' So now I'm here to help."

The nun not only took them and the body to the cemetery for a burial service, but she also gave them food and money for their trip home.[2]

Angels Encourage Believers

The apostle Paul was a prisoner on a ship en route to Rome during a severe storm. Everyone despaired, for they had been a long time without food. But Paul encouraged them all when he said that an angel had told him, "Do not be afraid, Paul. You must stand trial before Caesar; and God has graciously given you the lives of all who sail with you" (Acts 27:24).

When the late president of Wheaton College, Dr. V. Raymond Edman, and his wife were young missionaries in Ecuador, fanatical opponents often insulted them and even threw stones at them.

One day someone knocked on the gate.

Edman opened it cautiously and saw an indigenous woman in native dress.

She smiled and asked, "Are you the people who have come to tell us about the living God?"

"Yes, we are," he said.

Raising her hand, she prayed that they would receive courage and joy and that many would obey the gospel. "God bless you," she said, then bowed and quickly left.

Although Edman searched nearby streets to thank her, she was gone, and he never saw her again. He believed that God had sent an angel to encourage them.[3]

Angels Protect Believers

Jesus gave credence to the idea that angels protect humans when he said, "See that you do not despise one of these little ones. For I tell you that their angels in heaven always see the face of my Father in heaven" (Matthew 18:10).

Angels not only guard children but also all believers. God says that he "will command his angels concerning you to guard you in all your ways" (Psalm 91:11). "The angel of the Lord encamps around those who fear him, and he delivers them" (Psalm 34:7).

King Darius was forced to throw the prophet Daniel into a den of snarling lions. When the king checked on him in the morning, Daniel said, "My God sent his angel, and he shut the mouths of the lions" (Daniel 6:22).

In the early church, Jewish leaders arrested the apostles and imprisoned them. "But during the night an angel of the Lord opened the doors of the jail and brought them out" (Acts 5:19).

Later, King Herod put Peter in prison and commanded that guards bind him with chains. The night before his trial, the prisoner slept between two soldiers, and two sentries stood guard at the gate.

Suddenly, an angel appeared in Peter's cell and touched his chains, causing them to fall off. He told the apostle to get dressed and follow him. After they whisked past the guards, the heavy gate opened automatically, much to Peter's amazement. He followed the angel down one street before the heavenly being disappeared.

Peter later told his praying friends, "Now I know without a doubt that the Lord has sent his angel and rescued me from Herod's clutches and from everything the Jewish people were hoping would happen" (Acts 12:11).

On a dark and rainy night in 1947, my missionary friend, Walter Jespersen, arrived with a load of baggage at the bus station in Suyung, China. Leaving his large items locked in the station, he hired several young boys to carry small bags to the mission house. Splashing through the deserted streets in the rain, he prayed for God's protection for himself and his supplies.

Suddenly, a well-dressed Chinese gentleman appeared out of the darkness and walked beside Walter. "The carriers could disappear down these alleys," he said. "Count your bags, and I'll keep my eyes on them for you."

When they reached the gate, the man said, "Count your bags again to be sure they're all here."

Walter did so and unlocked the gate. He and the boys set the baggage inside. Then he turned to thank the kind gentleman and to offer him a tip. But he had disappeared, and Walter never saw him again. Walter thanked God for sending an apparent angel to protect him and his goods.[4]

Pastor and evangelist L. W. Northrup in his book, *Encounters with Angels*, tells about a Bible salesman in Norway descending a steep mountain with his heavy pack. Frightened at one dangerous place, he asked God to send an angel to go with him.

When he reached a cottage in the valley, a man and his wife said, "We watched you going down that awful trail. But what happened to the man who was with you?"

The Bible salesman had no companion, so he knew that God had sent an angel to protect him.[5]

John G. Paton, a missionary in the New Hebrides Islands, told a thrilling true story about God's protecting angels. One dark night, the Patons watched hostile natives with flaming torches surround their home, apparently intent on setting it on fire and killing them. Falling on their knees, the husband and wife prayed through the terror-filled night for God's deliverance. Amazingly, the attackers left early the next morning without doing them harm.

A year later when the chief became a believer, Paton asked him what kept him and his men from burning down their house and killing them that night.

The chief asked, "Who were all those men you had with you?"

Paton replied, "There were no men, just my wife and I."

The chief explained that hundreds of big men in shining garments with drawn swords circled the house, so they were afraid to attack.

"Praise God!" Paton said. "He must have sent a whole legion of angels to protect us!" [6]

Angels in Wartimes

During times of war, angels seem to be especially protective of believers. Author Hope Price, in her book, *Angels: True Stories of How They Touch Our Lives*, wrote that during a German blitz over London during World War II, Donavan and Doris Cox prayed for protection. Later, he saw a huge angel hovering over their house. In the night, they heard a loud explosion above them but knew that they were safe and went back to sleep.

The next morning, a street warden told them that he saw a parachute bomb explode in midair over their house. Later, a firewatcher told them the same thing. [7]

Price also told about amazing events during World War I that occurred near the town of Mons, Belgium, between the German and Allied troops in August 23–24, 1914.

Hearing that their troops were under special attack, leaders throughout Britain called for days of prayer, and praying people filled the churches.

The German cavalry advanced into Belgium and attacked the vastly outnumbered British troops. Knowing they could be annihilated, the soldiers felt helpless as the enemy galloped towards them. But several Englishmen saw a whole troop of angels between them and the enemy.

Suddenly, the German horses turned around and fled, with their men in great disorder.

Four years later in July 1918, leaders in both England and the US called for days of prayer.

German prisoners of war later told the Allies that they saw a vast cavalry of men in white uniforms riding white horses. Led by a distinguished officer with hair like gold, the white cavalry advanced like an incoming tide on a beach and passed right through enemy gunfire without harm.

The German army was panic-stricken. Whimpering like children, the men turned around and ran, throwing away anything that hindered their flight. Later, a German officer told his English captors that he knew then that they had lost the war. The "White Cavalry" had beaten them.[8]

In her book, *Tell No Man*, Adela Rogers St. John wrote that a celebration after World War II honored Air Chief Marshall Lord Hugh Dowding. King George VI, Prime Minister Winston Churchill, and other dignitaries were there. In a speech, the Air Chief Marshall told how their small air force saved Britain from invasion and defeat. His men rarely slept, and their planes flew nonstop.

During one mission when the pilots were either incapacitated or dead, their planes kept flying and fighting. Airmen in other planes saw figures at the controls, and the Air Chief Marshall believed they were angels.[9]

Angels Carry Believers to Heaven

A godly beggar named Lazarus "died and the angels carried him to Abraham's side," another way of referring to paradise (Luke 16:22). So too angels apparently carry believers to heaven when they die.

My friend Jane Dawson was dying of bone-marrow cancer. One morning she and her husband, Bus, awoke early. As they prayed together, committing themselves to the Lord and his will, a bright glow filled the room.

"Do you hear angels singing that beautiful music?" she asked.

"No," Bus answered. "What are they singing?"

"They're all songs we know."

Soon she lifted her head and asked, "Who's that standing at the foot of the bed? She's all in white."

"Is it Till Fell?" Bus asked. Their friend and colleague came by each day in her white nurse's uniform.

Jane smiled. "No, it's not Till."

Bus knelt beside Jane and held her hand. "It must be your guardian angel."

"Yes," she said. She breathed slowly and then was gone. A deep peace filled the room.

On another occasion, Dan Weaver's mother-in-law, Kay Pittman, was dying in her home in Waxhaw, North Carolina. Her daughter Peggy, a nurse, cared for her.

One day Kay gazed toward the foot of her bed and said,

"Look at them!" She paused. "They're so many!" Her voice faltered, and she choked up.

"Who, Mother?" Peggy asked.

"The angels . . . They're so nice." She turned to Peggy. "I want to ask them . . ." She groped for her thoughts, struggling to verbalize them. "I don't know if they'll understand . . . What are they doing? . . . You ask them."

"They don't talk to me, Mother," Peggy said gently. "Maybe the Lord sent them to be your companions."

Kay smiled and nodded.

Later, from the other room, Peggy heard her mother talking with her new friends. Not long after, they escorted her to Glory.

Just Think

Angels may provide for us, convey God's messages to us, guide and help us, encourage us, protect us, and finally will carry us to our heavenly home.

There we'll join the thousands upon thousands of angels singing praises to God around his throne. Oh, what a day that will be!

Angels, from the Realms of Glory

Angels, from the realms of glory,
Wing your flight o'er all the earth;
Ye who sang creation's story,
Now proclaim Messiah's birth.
Come and worship, come and worship,
Worship Christ, the newborn King.

Shepherds, in the field abiding,
Watching o'er your flocks by night,

God with man is now residing;
Yonder shines the infant Light;
Come and worship, come and worship,
Worship Christ, the newborn King.

—James Montgomery (1771–1854)

CHAPTER 11
WHAT WERE SAINTS' LAST WORDS?

Colors fade, temples crumble, empires fall, but wise words endure.

—Edward L. Thorndike

Today hospice and medical personnel give dying people morphine or other drugs to ease pain, and sedated patients silently slip out into eternity.

But before this type of palliative care was available, believers often said important last words or saw remarkable sights as they approached the gates of Glory. Consider the following:

Francis Asbury, English circuit-riding preacher, one of the first two bishops of the Methodist Episcopal Church in the US, said on his deathbed, "My eyes fail . . . But whether health, life, or death, good is the will of the Lord: I will trust Him; yes, and will praise Him; He is the strength of my heart and my portion forever—Glory! Glory! Glory!"[1]

Mrs. Charles Cowman, a missionary with her husband, Charles, was the author/compiler of the well-known devotional *Streams in the Desert.* On her deathbed, she asked, "Don't you see Jesus? He has a crown of pure gold on his head." Later, she said, "Last night I walked up the mountain with Jesus. Just Jesus and I. There will come the time when I take the last step."[2]

Jonathan Edwards was a pastor, theologian, evangelist, and author. On his deathbed, he looked around and said, "Now where is Jesus of Nazareth, my true and never-failing Friend?" To his family, his last utterance was, "Trust in God, and you need not fear."[3]

Jim Elliott, missionary and martyr, wrote in his journal, "He is no fool who gives what he cannot keep to gain what he cannot lose."[4] His wife, author Elisabeth, told the story of Jim's and his companions' martyrdoms in her book *Through Gates of Splendor*.

Billy Graham was a world evangelist and author. During his last days, he told his son, Franklin, that when he got to heaven, the first thing he would ask the Lord was, "Why did you choose a farmer's son from North Carolina to reach so many people for Christ?"[5]

Frances Ridley Havergal was an English poet and writer of such hymns as "Take My Life and Let It Be." On her deathbed, she said, "Beautiful! Too good to be true. Splendid to be so near the gates of heaven!"[6]

John Hyde, called "Praying Hyde," was a missionary in India who became well known for his prayer ministry. Just before he died, he called out, "Bol, Yisu Masih, Ki Jai!" ["Shout the victory of Jesus Christ!"][7]

Isobel Kuhn, missionary to China and Thailand, was the well-known author of such books as *By Searching* and *In the Arena*. When dying, she wrote: "The great end, *that I may know Him,* will be granted. We shall be clasped in His arms, we shall rest on His bosom with the impurities of our earth-clogged life gone forever."[8]

Eric Liddell, Scottish Olympic Gold medalist runner, was portrayed in the movie, *Chariots of Fire.* A missionary in China, he died of a brain tumor in a Japanese concentration camp during World War II. Near the end, he explained about full commitment to Christ to a young friend then whispered, "Annie, it's complete surrender."[9]

Henrietta Mears, dynamic American Christian educator, evangelist, founder of Gospel Light Press, and author of *What the Bible Is All About,* said, "What will I do when I get to heaven? Well, I am going to ask the Lord to show me around. I'll want to get in a rocket ship to inspect all the galaxies he has made. And maybe he will give me a planet of my own, so that I can start building something. Oh, it's going to be so wonderful!"[10]

Dwight L. Moody, American evangelist, founded Moody Church, the Moody Bible Institute, and Moody Press in Chicago, as well as Northfield School and Mount Hermon School in Massachusetts. Before he died, he said, "Earth recedes; heaven opens before me . . . If this is death, it is sweet. There is no valley here. God is calling me, and I must go."[11]

Andrew Murray, South African missionary, pastor, and author of popular devotional books, such as *With Christ in the School of Prayer,* said to his daughter before dying, "Have faith in God, my child. Do not doubt Him."[12]

John Newton, preacher and author of such hymns as, "Amazing Grace," said, "My dear friends, my memory is almost gone. But there are two things that I can still remember perfectly well. I can remember what a great sinner I was, and I can remember what a great Savior Christ Jesus is!"[13]

Hudson Taylor, founder and director of the China

Inland Mission (now Overseas Missionary Fellowship). On his deathbed, he said regarding prayer, "There is nothing small, and there is nothing great; only God is great, and we should trust Him fully."[14]

Corrie ten Boom was a prisoner in a Nazi concentration camp during World War II, speaker, and author. Before undergoing surgery, she said, "The best is yet to be. Now I might go Home to see Jesus face to face. From service good to service best. What joyful work there would be for me in heaven!"[15]

Charles Wesley, brother of John Wesley, was a preacher, evangelist, and the writer of 3,000 hymns, such as "O for a Thousand Tongues" and "Jesus, Lover of My Soul." Not long before his death, he dictated these words to his wife: "Jesus, my only hope thou art, / Strength of my failing flesh and heart; / Oh, could I catch a smile from thee, / And drop into eternity!"[16]

John Wesley was an English preacher, theologian, author, and a founder of Methodism with his brother Charles. Just before his death, a friend offered to write for him and asked what he should write. Wesley said, "Nothing but that God is with us."[17]

Just Think

We have the privilege of following in the train of these godly men and women, as Reginald Heber's hymn describes:

The Son of God Goes Forth to War

The Son of God goes forth to war
A kingly crown to gain.
His blood-red banner streams afar;
Who follows in His train?

Who best can drink His cup of woe,
Triumphant over pain,
Who patient bears his cross below—
He follows in His train.

A noble army, men and boys,
The matron and the maid,
Around the Savior's throne rejoice
In robes of light arrayed;
They climbed the steep ascent of heav'n
Through peril, toil, and pain.
O God, to us may grace be giv'n
To follow in their train!

—Reginald Heber (1783–1826)

Chapter 12

How Do We Get to Heaven?

Angels take us to heaven so we won't have to make the journey alone. God sends His heavenly escorts to lead us home.[1]

—David Jeremiah

My first husband, John Lawless, and I were shocked when an oncologist discovered that he had colorectal cancer. Because it had already metastasized to his liver, the doctor recommended immediate treatments. "Otherwise," he said, "I'll give you three to six months to live. Your case is terminal."

John had been so vigorous and healthy all his life that he figured he didn't need colonoscopies or even yearly checkups. He was always there for me, always able to do anything. I treasured him for not only giving me my first home when I'd been homeless but also for our fifty-three enjoyable years together. *What will I ever do without him?* I wondered.

After we talked about the situation, John decided to start the treatments. He wanted to spend more time with me as well as with our son, Ken, his wife, Fran, and our three young grandsons—Johnny, Joey, and Jeffrey.

John also felt he needed to teach me a few things he had always taken care of, such as, finances and putting gas in the car. One time I didn't park to his liking. Looking up, he said, "Lord, she's not ready yet!"

Early one morning, I crawled out of bed and gazed at a spectacular sky. The blue Cascade Mountains were etched against splashes of magenta, rose, and apricot.

"John," I called, "come and see!"

He got up and put his arm around my shoulders as we watched the sun climb out of the horizon in a blaze of glory.

I sighed when the show ended. "If earth can be this glorious," I asked, "what will heaven be like?"

He smiled. "I don't know, but we should find out, since I'm going there soon."

So in our devotional times together in the mornings, we read Scripture passages about heaven, which gave us hope and encouragement. In the evenings, we read good biographies, novels, and poetry together.

Soon our lives revolved around radiation, chemo, and doctors' appointments. At home, John spent most of his time in bed or on a recliner. Our beautiful black-and-white cat, Patches, climbed up on his chest and gave him special purring treatments.

After three years of that regimen, John decided to stop chemo. "All it does is put me in bed," he said. "I want to enjoy you and the family as long as I'm able."

He regained limited strength and tried to do something useful every day, such as pulling weeds in our garden. We played board games with our grandsons, and he taught Johnny, the eldest, to play chess.

But all too soon, John began hospice care. At our family Easter dinner, our daughter-in-law, Fran, hovered over him, cutting up a small portion of ham and scalloped potatoes for him. He nibbled a few bites then returned to bed. The next morning, he drank a little juice and part of a smoothie—the last nourishment he would ever take.

Knowing I was not strong enough to care for John's weakening body around the clock, the concerned hospice nurse called our son Ken at his fire station. "I think you should be here from now on," she said. "Can you get off work?"

Ken immediately moved in and lovingly cared for his dad. He could easily lift and move him when needed.

Since John was a reserved New Englander, he didn't often express his love in words. But as our son and I were sitting beside his bed one day, he suddenly rose up on one elbow and said, "Ken, I want you to know how much I love you! I'm so proud that you've turned out to be such a fine young man."

Ken rushed over to hug John and said through his tears, "Oh, Dad, I love you so much too! Thanks for being such a wonderful father."

Later, Fran took the children to stay with relatives, and she moved in as well. Together they changed the sheets while John was in bed, turned him over so he wouldn't get bedsores, and administered medications. Ken even took the night watch.

Before long, John lost his power of speech and slept most of the time. When he was awake, Ken read the Bible to him, I sang his favorite hymns, and we all prayed with him.

One April afternoon, we felt that John was slipping away. We watched gray clouds part and the sun's golden rays streak the sky, as if to welcome him.

As I stared out the window, I knew he was on his way. Then I whispered, "He's gone."

Ken, Fran, and I hugged each other and wept. But in our grief, we were confident that the angels had carried John to his heavenly Father's home.

Henry van Dyke (1852–1933), American author, educator, and clergyman, beautifully described the process of dying:

I am standing upon the seashore.
A ship at my side spreads her white sails to the morning breeze
And starts for the blue ocean.
She is an object of beauty and strength.
I stand and watch her until at length she hangs like a speck of white cloud
Just where the sea and sky come to mingle with each other.
Then, someone at my side says, "There, she is gone!"
Gone where? Gone from my sight. That is all.
She is just as large in mast and hull
And spar as she was when she left my side.
And she is just as able to bear her
Load of living freight to her destined port.
Her diminished size is in me, not in her.
Just at the moment when someone
At my side says, "There, she is gone!"
There are other eyes watching her coming
And other voices ready to take up the glad shout, "Here she comes!"
And that is dying.[2]

The apostle Paul wrote these comforting words near his life's end: "We know that if the earthly tent we live in is destroyed, we have a building from God, an eternal house in heaven, not built by human hands" (2 Corinthians 5:1).

How to Get Ready

While we're still on earth, we need to get ready to leave at any time. We don't know when death will take us, whether we're old or young. Here are some suggestions:

First of all, if you haven't already done so, ask Jesus Christ to forgive your sins and to become your Savior and Lord. This will ensure that heaven is your final destination.

Second, read your Bible daily. Do so when your mind is fresh, usually in the morning. In later years, I've been reading two chapters in the Old Testament, two in the New Testament, and several psalms each day. It's helpful to pray as you read, asking God to make his Word real to you.

Third, pray daily—by yourself or with your spouse or another person. Start by praising God then pray for your family members, for your spiritual leaders, for the sick and needy, for our country, or whatever the Lord prompts you to pray for.

Fourth, provide financially for your family. Then consider supporting Christian ministries that help you grow spiritually, as well as worthy charities, as you see fit.

Fifth, take care of practical matters. Let your close family members know about your will; living will; Social Security number; medical information; banking, credit cards, insurance policies; real-estate investments; and funeral and burial arrangements. Don't leave them hunting for such information after you've gone.

The Best Is Yet to Be

Just think: In this book, we have learned that when we reach heaven, we will have a beautiful home, new bodies, no pain or sorrow, useful service, and crowns of reward. We'll know our friends and families, angels will carry us there, and we will join them in praising and worshipping God the Father and our Lord Jesus Christ for all eternity.

We will have reached our heavenly home, and our questions will all be answered!

Amazing Grace

Amazing grace! How sweet the sound,
That saved a wretch like me!
I once was lost, but now am found,
Was blind, but now I see.

When we've been there ten thousand years,
Bright shining as the sun,
We've no less days to sing God's praise
Than when we first begun.

—John Newton (1725–1807)

The Other Side

This isn't death; it's glory!
It isn't dark; it's light!
It isn't stumbling, groping,
Or even faith—it's sight!
This isn't grief; it's having
The last tear wiped away.
It's sunrise; it's the morning
Of my eternal day!

It isn't even praying;
It's speaking face to face;
It's listening, and it's glimpsing
The wonders of His grace.
This is the end of pleading
For strength to bear my pain.
Not even pain's dark memory
Will ever live again.

How did I bear the earth life
Before I came up higher,
Before my soul was granted
Its every deep desire,
Before I knew this rapture
Of meeting face-to-face,
The One who sought me, saved me,
And kept me by His grace?

—Martha Snell Nicholson

ENDNOTES

Chapter 1: WHAT IS HEAVEN LIKE?

1. Anne Graham Lotz, *Heaven: My Father's House* (Nashville: W Publishing, 2001, 2014), 11.

2. To read more about Newell's work in the Philippines, see Len Newell, *Headhunters' Encounter with God: An Ifugao Adventure* (New York: iUniverse, 2007).

3. Al Bryant, comp., ed., *Climbing the Heights* (Grand Rapids: Zondervan, 1956), 202.

4. David Jeremiah, *Answers to Your Questions About Heaven* (San Diego: Turning Point for God, 2013, 2015), 112.

5. Randy Alcorn, *Heaven* (Wheaton, IL: Tyndale, 2004), 242.

6. Ibid.

7. Jeremiah, 113.

8. John F. Walvoord, *The Revelation of Jesus Christ* (Chicago: Moody Publishers, 1966, 1989), 325.

9. Don Baker, *Heaven: A Glimpse of Your Future Home* (Sisters, OR: Multnomah, 1983, 1986), 9.

10. Merrill C. Tenney, *Interpreting Revelation* (Grand Rapids: Eerdmans, 1957, 1970, 1988), 93.

Chapter 2: WHAT WILL WE BE LIKE IN HEAVEN?

1. David Jeremiah, *Answers to Your Questions About Heaven* (San Diego: Turning Point for God, 2013, 2015), 96.

2. David Brian Winter, *Hereafter: What Happens after Death?* (Wheaton, IL: Shaw, 1972, 1973), 57.

3. Jeremiah, 72.

4. Randy Alcorn, *In Light of Eternity: Perspectives on Heaven* (Colorado Springs: Waterbrook, 1999), 48.

5. Don Baker, *Heaven: A Glimpse of Your Future Home* (Sisters, OR: Multnomah, 1983, 1986), 13.

Chapter 3: WHERE IS HEAVEN?

1. D. L. Moody, *Heaven: Where It Is, Its Inhabitants, and How to Get There* (Burlington, ON: Inspirational Promotions, n.d.), 15.

2. David Jeremiah, *Answers to Your Questions About Heaven* (San Diego: Turning Point for God, 2013, 2015), 18.

3. Charles R. Swindoll, *Growing Deep in the Christian Life: Returning to Our Roots* (Portland, OR: Multnomah, 1986), 271.

4. James T. Jeremiah, *The Place Called Heaven* (Arlington Heights, IL: Regular Baptist, 1991, 1994; San Diego: Turning Point for God, 2005), 13.

5. Don Baker, *Heaven: A Glimpse of Your Future Home* (Portland, OR: Multnomah, 1983, 1986), 5.

6. John R. Rice, *Bible Facts About Heaven: Sweet Home of the Lord Jesus and Departed Saints* (Murfreesboro, TN: Sword of the Lord, 1940), 14.

7. Moody, 15.

8. Ibid.

9. David Jeremiah, 20.

10. Ibid., 21.

11. *The Holy Bible, New King James Version* (Nashville: Thomas Nelson/Word, 1982, 1997), 785.

12. *The NIV Study Bible* (Grand Rapids: Zondervan, 1985), 1061.

13. *The Ryrie Study Bible* (Chicago: Moody Press, 1986, 1995), 873.

14. David Jeremiah, *Revealing the Mysteries of Heaven* (San Diego: Turning Point for God, 2017), 17.

15. Robert Roy Britt, "Huge Hole Found in the Universe," 23 August 2007, <http.//.www.space.com/427-huge-hole-universe.html.>

16. Ibid.

17. Ibid.

Chapter 4: WHAT IS NOT IN HEAVEN?

1. E. M. Bounds, *A Place Called Heaven* (New Kensington, PA: Whitaker, 1985, 2003), 24.

2. Merrill C. Tenney, *Interpreting Revelation* (Grand Rapids: Eerdmans, 1957, 1970, 1988), 93.

3. John Woodbridge, ed., *More Than Conquerors: Portraits of Believers from All Walks of Life* (Chicago: Moody Publishers, 1992), 195–196.

4. Sam Storms, "Heaven: The Eternal Increase of Joy," *Decision*, May 2007, 11–13.

5. Al Bryant, comp., ed., *1,000 New Illustrations* (Grand Rapids: Zondervan, 1957), 112.

Chapter 5: WHAT WILL WE DO IN HEAVEN?

1. Don Baker, *Heaven: A Glimpse of Your Future Home* (Sisters, OR: Multnomah, 1983, 1986), 16.

2. David Jeremiah, *Answers to Your Questions About Heaven* (San Diego: Turning Point for God, 2013, 2015), 46.

3. James T. Jeremiah, *The Place Called Heaven* (Arlington Heights, IL: Regular Baptist, 1991, 1994; Turning Point for God, 2005), 47.

4. Wilbur E. Nelson, "Glorious Truths About Heaven," *The Grace Broadcaster*, April 1966, 3.

5. Baker, 16.

6. J. Oswald Sanders, *Heaven: Better by Far: Answers to Questions About the Believer's Final Hope* (Grand Rapids: Discovery, 1993, 2013), 102.

7. Dallas Willard, *The Divine Conspiracy: Rediscovering Our Hidden Life in God* (San Francisco: Harper, 1997, 1998), 378.

Chapter 6: WILL WE BE REWARDED IN HEAVEN?

1. J. Oswald Sanders, *Heaven, Better by Far: Answers to Questions About the Believer's Final Hope* (Grand Rapids: Discovery, 1993, 2013), 81.

2. Robert D. Foster, *The Navigator* (Colorado Springs: NavPress, 1980, 2012), 2.

3. Roger Martin, *R. A. Torrey: Apostle of Certainty* (Murfreesboro, TN: Sword of the Lord, 1976, 2000), 167.

4. Kirsopp Lake, ed., trans., *The Martyrdom of Polycarp* (Whitefish, MT: Kessinger, 2005), n.p.

5. John Woodbridge, ed., *More Than Conquerors: Portraits of Believers from All Walks of Life* (Chicago: Moody Publishers, 1992), 174.

6. Ibid., 180.

7. Nancy E. Robbins, *God's Madcap: The Story of Amy Carmichael* (Fort Washington, PA: Christian Literature Crusade, 1962; Cambridge, UK: Lutterworth, 1975), 92–95.

8. Amy Carmichael, *Toward Jerusalem* (London: Society for Promoting Christian Knowledge, 1961, 1987; Fort Washington, PA: Christian Literature Crusade, 1988), 108.

Chapter 7: WILL WE KNOW EACH OTHER IN HEAVEN?

1. James T. Jeremiah, *The Place Called Heaven* (Arlington Heights, IL: Regular Baptist, 1991, 1994; San Diego: Turning Point for God, 2005), 25.

2. David Jeremiah, *Answers to Your Questions About Heaven* (San Diego: Turning Point, 2013, 2015), 97.

3. J. Oswald Sanders, *Heaven: Better by Far: Answers to Questions About the Believer's Final Hope* (Grand Rapids: Discovery, 1993, 2013), 35, 38.

Chapter 8: CAN PEOPLE IN HEAVEN OBSERVE US?

1. Randy Alcorn, *In Light of Eternity: Perspectives on Heaven* (Colorado Springs: Waterbrook, 1999), 97–98.

2. Catherine Marshall, *Meeting God at Every Turn* (Carmel, NY: Guideposts, 1980; New York: Bantam, 1982; Grand Rapids: Chosen/Baker, 2002), 104–105.

3. Ibid.

4. John F. MacArthur, *The Glory of Heaven: The Truth About Heaven, Angels, and Eternal Life* (Wheaton, IL: Crossway, 1996, 1998, 2013), 246.

5. Robert Jamison, A. R. Fausset, and David Brown, *Commentary: Practical and Explanatory on the Whole Bible* (Grand Rapids: Zondervan, 1961, 1963, 1999), 1437.

6. Alcorn, 97–98.

Chapter 9: WHO ARE ANGELS, AND WHAT DO THEY DO IN HEAVEN?

1. *Guideposts* editors, comp., *Angels in Our Midst* (New York: Doubleday/ Guideposts, 1993), 62.

2. Steve Saint, "The Untold Story of the Auca Murders," *Christian Reader,* March/April 1997, 102.

3. Billy Graham, *Angels: God's Secret Agents* (New York: Doubleday, 1975; Nashville: Thomas Nelson, 1995), 18.

4. David Jeremiah, *Answers to Your Questions About Heaven* (San Diego: Turning Point for God, 2013, 2015), 58.

5._____, *What the Bible Says About Angels* (Sisters, OR: Multnomah, 1996), 154.

6. Ibid.

Chapter 10: WHAT DO ANGELS DO ON EARTH?

1. David Jeremiah, *Answers to Your Questions About Heaven* (San Diego: Turning Point for God, 2013, 2015), 83.

2. Richard E. Elkins, and Agnes Lawless Elkins, *Time and*

Again: God's Sovereignty in the Lives of Two Bible Translators in the Philippines (Bloomington, IN: WestBow, 2011), 123–124.

3. V. Raymond Edman, "I, Too, Saw an Angel," *The Alliance Witness*, December 22, 1965.

4. A. C. Lawless, *Under His Wings: Protected by God in China* (Manila: Action International, 2003), 169–170.

5. L. W. Northrup, *Encounters with Angels* (Wheaton, IL: Tyndale, 1988), 38.

6. Billy Graham, *Angels: God's Secret Agents* (New York: Doubleday, 1975; Nashville: Thomas Nelson, 1995), 3.

7. Hope Price, *Angels: True Stories of How They Touch Our Lives* (Carmel, NY: Guideposts, 1993), 7–8.

8. Ibid., 85–87, 93–94.

9. Graham, 163–164.

Chapter 11: WHAT WERE SAINTS' LAST WORDS?

1. Charles Ludwig, *Francis Asbury: God's Circuit Rider* (Fenton, MI: Mott Media, 1984), 183.

2. B. H. Pearson, *The Vision Lives: A Profile of Mrs. Charles E. Cowman* (Los Angeles: Cowman, 1961), 339–340.

3. Iain H. Murray, *Jonathan Edwards: A New Biography* (Carlisle, PA: The Banner of Truth, 1987), 441.

4. Elisabeth Elliott, *Shadow of the Almighty: The Life and Testament of Jim Elliott* (Grand Rapids: Zondervan, 1958), 247.

5. Franklin Graham, *Decision,* Commemorative Edition, 2018, 3.

6. Wesley L. Duewel, *Heroes of the Holy Life: Biographies of Fully Devoted Followers of Christ* (Grand Rapids: Zondervan, 2002), 89.

7. Basil Miller, *Praying Hyde: A Man of Prayer* (Grand Rapids: Zondervan, 1943), 130.

8. Isobel Kuhn, *In the Arena* (Chicago: Moody Press, 1958), 221.

9. Sally Magnusson, *The Flying Scotsman* (New York: Quartet Books, 1981, 1987; Mt. Pleasant, SC: History Press, 2007), 169.

10. Ethel May Baldwin and David V. Benson, *Henrietta Mears and How She Did It!* (Grand Rapids: Regal/Baker, 1980), 259.

11. William R. Moody, *The Life of D. L. Moody by His Son* (Murfreesboro, TN: Sword of the Lord, 1930; Charleston, SC: Nabu, 2011), 552.

12. Leona Choy, *Andrew Murray: Apostle of Abiding Love* (Fort Washington, PA: Christian Literature Crusade, 1978, 2004), 251.

13. Kay Marshall Strom, *John Newton: The Angry Sailor* (Chicago: Moody Publishers, 1984), 124.

14. Dr. and Mrs. Howard Taylor, *Hudson Taylor and the China Inland Mission: The Growth of a Work of God* (Singapore: Overseas Missionary Fellowship, 1918, 1988), 616.

15. Carole C. Carlson, *Corrie ten Boom: Her Life, Her Faith* (Old Tappan, NJ: Fleming H. Revell, 1983), 2.

16. Arnold A. Dallimore, *A Heart Set Free: The Life of Charles Wesley* (Westchester, IL: Crossway, 1988), 250.

17. Basil Miller, *John Wesley* (Minneapolis: Bethany, 1943), 138–139.

Chapter 12: HOW DO WE GET TO HEAVEN?

1. David Jeremiah, *Answers to Your Questions About Heaven* (San Diego: Turning Point for God, 2013), 36.

2. Linda Slaton Anderson and Seth C. Anderson, *The Joy Guide: Keys to Happiness, Health, and Prosperity* (Bloomington, IN: Inspiring Voices, 2012), 22.

BIBLIOGRAPHY

Alcorn, Randy. *Heaven*. Wheaton, IL: Tyndale, 2004.

_____. *In Light of Eternity: Perspectives on Heaven*. Colorado Springs: Waterbrook, 1999.

Anderson, Linda Slaton, and Seth C. Anderson. *The Joy Guide: Keys to Happiness, Health, and Prosperity*. Bloomington, IN: Inspiring Voices, 2012.

Baker, Don. *Heaven: A Glimpse of Your Future Home*. Sisters, OR: Multnomah, 1983, 1986.

Baldwin, Ethel May, and David V. Benson. *Henrietta Mears and How She Did It!* Grand Rapids: Regal/Baker, 1980.

Bounds, E. M. *A Place Called Heaven*. New Kensington, PA: Whitaker, 1985, 2003.

Britt, Robert Roy. "Huge Hole Found in the Universe." 23 August 2007. <http.//www.space.com/427–huge–hole–universe.html.>

Bryant, Al, comp., ed. *Climbing the Heights*. Grand Rapids: Zondervan, 1956.

_____. *1,000 New Illustrations*. Grand Rapids: Zondervan, 1957.

Bunyan, John. *The Pilgrim's Progress*. Virginia Beach: CBN University Press, 1978.

Carmichael, Amy. *Toward Jerusalem*. London: Society for Promoting Christian Knowledge, 1961, 1987; Fort Washington, PA: Christian Literature Crusade, 1988.

Carlson, Carole C. *Corrie ten Boom: Her Life, Her Faith.* Old Tappan, NJ: Fleming H. Revell, 1983.

Choy, Leona. *Andrew Murray: Apostle of Abiding Love.* Fort Washington, PA: Christian Literature Crusade, 1978, 2004.

Dallimore, Arnold A. *A Heart Set Free: The Life of Charles Wesley.* Westchester, IL: Crossway, 1988.

Duewel, Wesley L. *Heroes of the Holy Life: Biographies of Fully Devoted Followers of Christ.* Grand Rapids: Zondervan, 2002.

Edman, V. Raymond. "I, Too, Saw an Angel." *The Alliance Witness,* December 22, 1965.

Elkins, Richard E., and Agnes Lawless Elkins. *Time and Again: God's Sovereignty in the Lives of Two Bible Translators in the Philippines.* Bloomington, IN: WestBow, 2011.

Elliott, Elisabeth, *Shadow of the Almighty: The Life and Testament of Jim Elliott.* Grand Rapids: Zondervan, 1958.

Foster, Robert D. *The Navigator.* Colorado Springs: NavPress, 1980, 2012.

Graham, Billy. *Angels: God's Secret Agents.* New York: Doubleday, 1975; Nashville: Thomas Nelson, 1995.

Graham, Franklin. *Decision.* Commemorative Edition, 2018.

Guideposts editors, comp. *Angels in Our Midst.* New York: Doubleday/Guideposts, 1993.

Jamieson, Robert, A. R. Fausset, and David Brown. *Commentary: Practical and Explanatory on the Whole Bible.* Grand Rapids: Zondervan, 1961, 1963, 1999.

Jeremiah, David. *Answers to Your Questions About Heaven.* San Diego: Turning Point for God, 2013, 2015.

_____. *Revealing the Mysteries of Heaven.* San Diego: Turning Point for God, 2017.

_____. *What the Bible Says About Angels.* Sisters, OR: Multnomah, 1996.

Jeremiah, James T. *The Place Called Heaven.* Arlington Heights, IL: Regular Baptist 1991, 1994; San Diego: Turning Point for God, 2005.

Kuhn, Isobel. *In the Arena.* Chicago: Moody Press, 1958.

Lake, Kirsopp, ed., trans. *The Martyrdom of Polycarp.* Whitefish, MT: Kessinger, 2005.

Lawless, A. C. *Under His Wings: Protected by God in China.* Manila: Action International, 2003.

Lotz, Anne Graham. *Heaven: My Father's House.* Nashville: W Publishing, 2001, 2014.

Ludwig, Charles. *Francis Asbury: God's Circuit Rider.* Fenton, MI: Mott Media, 1984.

MacArthur, John F. *The Glory of Heaven: The Truth About Heaven, Angels, and Eternal Life.* Wheaton, IL: Crossway, 1996, 1998, 2013.

MacDonald, Hope. *Letters from Heaven.* Colorado Springs: NavPress, 1998.

Magnusson, Sally. *The Flying Scotsman.* New York: Quartet Books, 1981, 1987; Mt. Pleasant, SC: History Press, 2007.

Marshall, Catherine. *Meeting God at Every Turn.* Carmel, NY: Guideposts, 1980; New York: Bantam, 1982; Grand Rapids: Chosen/Baker, 2002.

Martin, Roger. *R. A. Torrey: Apostle of Certainty.* Murfreesboro, TN: Sword of the Lord, 1976, 2000.

Miller, Basil. *John Wesley.* Minneapolis: Bethany, 1943.

_____. *Praying Hyde: A Man of Prayer.* Grand Rapids: Zondervan, 1943.

Moody, D. L. *Heaven: Where It Is, Its Inhabitants, and How to Get There.* Burlington, ON: Inspirational Promotions, n.d.

Moody, William R. *The Life of D. L. Moody by His Son.* Murfreesboro, TN: Sword of the Lord, 1930; Charleston, SC: Nabu, 2011.

Murray, Iain, H. *Jonathan Edwards: A New Biography.* Carlisle, PA: The Banner of Truth, 1987.

Nelson, Wilbur E. "Glorious Truths About Heaven." *The Grace Broadcaster,* April 1966.

Newell, Len. *Headhunters' Encounter with God: An Ifugao Adventure.* New York: iUniverse, 2007.

Northrup, L. W. *Encounters with Angels.* Wheaton, IL: Tyndale, 1988.

Pearson, B. H. *The Vision Lives: A Profile of Mrs. Charles E. Cowman.* Los Angeles: Cowman, 1961.

Pollock, John. *Moody: The Biography.* Chicago: Moody Publishers, 1983; Grand Rapids: Baker, 1997.

Price, Hope. *Angels: True Stories of How They Touch Our Lives.* Carmel, NY: Guideposts, 1993.

Rice, John R. *Bible Facts About Heaven: Sweet Home of the Lord Jesus and Departed Saints.* Murfreesboro, TN: Sword of the Lord, 1940.

Robbins, Nancy E. *God's Madcap: The Story of Amy Carmichael.* Fort Washington, PA: Christian Literature Crusade, 1962; Cambridge, UK: Lutterworth, 1975.

Saint, Steve. "The Untold Story of the Auca Murders." *Christian Reader,* March/April 1997.

Sanders, J. Oswald. *Heaven: Better by Far: Answers to Questions About the Believer's Final Hope.* Grand Rapids: Discovery, 1993, 2013.

Storms, Sam. "Heaven: The Eternal Increase of Joy." *Decision,* May 2007.

Strom, Kay Marshall. *John Newton: The Angry Sailor.* Chicago: Moody Publishers, 1984.

Swindoll, Charles R. *Growing Deep in the Christian Life: Returning to Our Roots.* Portland, OR: Multnomah, 1986.

Taylor, Dr. and Mrs. Howard. *Hudson Taylor and the China Inland Mission: The Growth of a Work of God.* Singapore: Overseas Missionary Fellowship, 1918, 1988.

Tenney, Merrill C. *Interpreting Revelation.* Grand Rapids: Eerdmans, 1957, 1970, 1988.

Walvoord, John F. *The Revelation of Jesus Christ.* Chicago: Moody Publishers, 1966, 1989.

Willard, Dallas. *The Divine Conspiracy: Rediscovering Our Hidden Life in God.* San Francisco: Harper, 1997, 1998.

Winter, David Brian. *Hereafter: What Happens after Death?* Wheaton, IL: Shaw, 1972, 1973.

Woodbridge, John, ed. *More Than Conquerors: Portraits of Believers from All Walks of Life.* Chicago: Moody Publishers, 1992.

About the Author

Agnes C. Lawless was one of founders of the Northwest Christian Writers Association and served on the board for several years as president and in other positions. She also edited its former newsletter, *The Northwest Christian Author*.

Agnes has authored or coauthored twelve nonfiction books and contributed to two writing books, as well as to several anthologies. Her articles have been published in a number of magazines, and she also has made a career of editing and proofreading books for publishers and individuals. Editors and writers often refer to her as "Flawless Lawless."

Agnes not only was an honor graduate of both Prairie Bible College and Seattle Pacific University, but she also appeared in *Who's Who Among Students in American Universities and College*. In addition, she did graduate work at Syracuse University in religious journalism, Hartford Seminary, and the University of North Dakota.

While in the Philippines with Wycliffe Bible Translators with her husband, John Lawless, she founded and taught in a school for missionary children. Returning to the States, she taught in the Northshore School District in Bothell, Washington. She later taught English grammar and writing at Northwest University in Kirkland, Washington.

Agnes grew up on Bainbridge Island in Washington State with five siblings. Her Scottish father, Allan Cunningham Sr., was the inventor and manufacturer of marine deck machinery, as well as his famous air whistles "heard 'round the world." Born in Ellensburg, Washington, her mother, Kathryn, spent her early years in Seattle, studied voice, and sang professionally for church services, weddings, and funerals.